WITHDRAWN

Equal Opportunity for Women in the Workplace: A Study of Corporate Disclosure

Kate Grosser
International Centre for Corporate Social Responsibility
Nottingham University Business School

Professor Carol Adams
Faculty of Law and Management
La Trobe University, Melbourne

Professor Jeremy Moon
International Centre for Corporate Social Responsibility
Nottingham University Business School

Certified Accountants Educational Trust (London)

ISBN: 978-1-85908-442-7

Contents

Abbreviations 4

Executive summary 5

1. Introduction 8

2. Data on gender equality/diversity 18

3. Why companies take action on gender equality 33

4. Why companies report externally 39

5. Barriers to external reporting 44

6. Processes of reporting 48

7. The future of reporting 54

8. Discussion and recommendations 57

Appendix 1: Examples of gender and diversity awards and benchmarks referenced in the sampled company reports 60

Appendix 2: Examples of CSR awards and benchmarks referenced in the sampled company reports 61

References 62

Abbreviations

ACTU	Australian Council of Trade Unions
ASX	Australian Stock Exchange
BiTC	Business in the Community
BRC	British Retail Consortium
CEO	Chief executive officer
CRE	Commission for Racial Equality
CSR	Corporate social responsibility
CSD	Corporate social disclosure
D&I	Diversity and inclusiveness
DTI	Department of Trade and Industry (UK)
ECRA	Ethical Consumer Research Association
EEOC	Equal Employment Opportunity Commission (US)
EOC	Equal Opportunities Commission (UK)
EOWA	Equal Opportunities for Women in the Workplace Agency (Australia)
EIRIS	Ethical Investment Research Service
GRI	Global Reporting Initiative
KPI	Key performance indicators
NGO	Non-governmental organisation
ON	Opportunity Now (UK)
S&P	Standard & Poor's
SRI	Socially Responsible Investment

Executive summary

INTRODUCTION

Today, equal opportunities management and reporting has real significance in corporate social responsibility (CSR) and socially responsible investment (SRI) criteria. Internationally, business, government and non-governmental organisations (NGOs) acknowledge that effective monitoring of equal opportunities and diversity in the workplace is an important part of improved human capital management and equality practice. The drive for transparency and accountability for such issues – including equal opportunities for women – has perhaps never been stronger.

ACCA has commissioned research to investigate public reporting on equal opportunities for women in the workplace among some of the largest employers in three national regulatory environments: the US, Australia and the UK. Although reporting by the leading companies is comparable in all three countries, collectively Australian companies are found to report less information on this issue than their UK and US counterparts. Across all three countries, findings suggest that the recent drive for greater CSR has become a major influence on the reporting of workplace gender issues, although regulation that obliges firms to report to government (in the US and Australia) has also played an important role in driving this agenda.

BACKGROUND AND CONTEXT

For different reasons, business, government and NGOs internationally have acknowledged the importance of monitoring and managing equal opportunities and diversity effectively, as part of improved human capital management and equalities practice. They have also recognised the importance of accountability for such issues, including equal opportunities for women, and the importance of public reporting. Moreover, equal opportunities management and reporting has acquired additional significance in recent developments in CSR reporting systems and SRI criteria.

This study compares research findings on how a sample of the largest companies in the UK, Australia and the US have publicly reported on equal opportunities for women in the workplace. It examines the different regulatory and voluntary frameworks relating to corporate reporting on gender equality in the workplace in these countries, and analyses the extent to which regulation and other drivers have encouraged and shaped public disclosure and accountability on this issue.

The aims of the research are:

- to ascertain the extent and nature of public reporting on women's employment issues in a sample of the largest Australian, UK and US companies

- to assess how such reporting of gender issues at the workplace has developed over the last decade in the UK (the country for which we had substantial prior data)

- to evaluate the impact of regulatory and voluntary approaches to equal opportunities reporting in each country

- to evaluate the extent and the ways in which CSR has become a driver of corporate social disclosure (CSD) on gender equality in the workplace

- to recommend steps for improving transparency on this issue.

The research comprises:

- an examination of both mandatory and voluntary reporting frameworks in each country

- content analysis of corporate annual reports and CSR reports for the year ending 1 February 2005 to 31 January 2006 and of company websites from February to June 2006

- in-depth interviews with managers in UK and Australian companies who were responsible for diversity issues with respect to women's employment and reporting thereon (March–June 2006).

Much of the prior research on corporate accountability for equal opportunities in the UK, where reporting on women's employment issues is voluntary, has focused on reporting in the annual report. Examining disclosures up until the mid 1990s, this research found that many companies reported their equal opportunity policies, but that there was little reporting of performance information and that summaries of data collected for internal purposes were rarely included. It was concluded that self-regulatory initiatives for disclosure had limited potential for improved accountability and that there was little alternative to regulation if we sought an improvement in accountability, and the opportunity to discover where inequality of opportunity lies.

Although none of the countries studied here has regulation to require public reporting, Australia and the US have different forms of reporting regulation on women's workplace issues, both of which require regular reporting to government. In contrast, the UK adopts an entirely voluntary approach.

Many analyses explain changing disclosure practices on gender and women's employment issues, particularly with reference to the changing social, political and economic context. The present study focuses on one recent contextual development, namely the new interest in CSR. CSR has been a relatively long-standing theme in the US, but the UK is now widely regarded as the current leader. Although CSR has also acquired new dynamism in Australia it still lags behind the UK and the US.

Generally, CSR has been associated with a dramatic growth in the reporting of companies' broad social impacts and responsibilities. Thus, in the last five years, over 90% of the FTSE 100 companies have made some report of their CSR. This reflects the assumption that a responsible company is one that reports its activities. There are now awards for social responsibility reporting, such as the annual ACCA Awards for Sustainability Reporting in a number of countries and regions.

Many explanatory accounts of the new enthusiasm for CSR identify market, civil society and government drivers. Market drivers for CSR arise from the greater inclusion of social criteria in the market decisions of consumers, employees, investors, and business customers. Civil society drivers reflect greater public interest in company behaviour – where, for example, NGOs may be both adversaries and partners of companies – along with media attention and general social expectations of business responsibility. Business associations and CSR coalitions assist companies in meeting these newly articulated expectations. Government drivers range from basic endorsement and support for CSR to 'soft regulation' to encourage more responsible business, eg through tax incentives, public procurement criteria. In this context, gender equality and diversity are increasingly defined as key CSR issues and companies that adopt best practice increasingly report on workplace gender issues.

The present study investigates the impacts of these different sorts of driver in explaining the levels and nature of developments in reporting of gender issues in the workplace among the largest employers in three national regulatory environments. The key findings are summarised below.

REPORTING PRACTICE

We found examples of detailed and extensive performance reporting on gender equality in the workplace in all three countries, as well as much reporting on programmes of actions on this issue.

Most performance reporting covers women's employment patterns/workplace profile. Reporting is much more limited when it comes to workplace practices such as recruitment, retention, and career development and training.

In many cases, companies report their progress over time on a number of gender issues identified as important to the company (eg women's representation in management).

Some issues prioritised by civil society and government are reported on (eg equal pay, litigation, sexual harassment and women's representation in non-traditional jobs), but only by a minority of companies.

Reporting on performance on workplace gender issues among UK companies has improved considerably over the last decade.

In all three countries, reporting is comparable among companies that have adopted best practice but, collectively, Australian companies report less information on this issue than their UK and US counterparts. US companies no longer report significantly more on the employment and advancement of women than UK companies.

The lack of comparable reporting systems and key performance indicators means that opportunities for meaningful comparisons and benchmarking between companies are very limited, even on the issues on which nearly all companies report, such as women's representation in management.

The problem of non-comparable data is one of the greatest barriers to improved reporting on this issue.

THE ROLE OF REGULATION

The regulatory obligation to report to government in Australia has driven monitoring and internal reporting on gender equality in all companies where this was not already a management focus. These developments have facilitated progress and external reporting. The regulation has also acted as a prompt, or catalyst, to alert companies to the business drivers for equal opportunities for women, which we found are also drivers of external reporting. In these ways regulation to report to government has been a driver of external reporting for several of our sample companies.

Data reported to government are sometimes used in public reporting (US and Australia) and the national average data published by government are used as benchmarks to report against by several US companies. The requirement to report to government has enabled civil society organisations and shareholders to call upon companies to increase their transparency on this issue by publishing this data.

Nonetheless, for Australian companies that already focused on this agenda before 1999, regulation to report to government has not been a major driver of reporting to the public.

THE ROLE OF CORPORATE SOCIAL RESPONSIBILITY

The socialised market drivers associated with the recent growth of CSR in general are also identified as critical to company action and reporting on gender issues, in particular those relating to current employees, potential recruits and investors.[1]

Likewise, civil society drivers for responsible business behaviour in the workplace were noted as additional motivations for reporting gender issues.

---

1. By socialised market drivers we mean the impact of new societal expectations of business with regard to social and environmental issues, as manifested through market actors such as employees, potential employees, investors, consumers and supply chains.

Companies report much more information on gender equality in their CSR reports and on their CSR websites than in their annual reports.

CSR reporting and benchmarking systems (eg the Global Reporting Initiative (GRI), Business in the Community (BiTC) CR Index, Opportunity Now (ON)) now encourage and inform reporting on gender issues.

Company CSR departments and committees, in collaboration with diversity and HR departments, play a central role in identifying stakeholder interests and editing and producing CSR reports.

It appears that CSR has become a major influence on the reporting of workplace gender issues.

IMPLICATIONS AND RECOMMENDATIONS

Both legislative and non-legislative mechanisms are important in the process of improving equal opportunities monitoring and reporting to the public. Previous studies have recommended mandatory public reporting, and it seems that this approach may well still be necessary. We found that regulation to report to government has played a critical role in driving action and reporting on gender issues in some companies, suggesting that regulation for broader public reporting, if ever enacted, could have a similar affect, as suggested by previous research (eg SIRAN 2005). Given the lack of such regulation in the countries we looked at, our study could not test the efficacy of such legislation, and our interviewees had mixed views on this issue.

Significantly, we also found that market, civil society and government drivers for greater CSR have been very influential with regard to company action and public reporting on gender issues. Not only did our interviewees tell us this, but we found that reporting has improved significantly in the UK (the country for which we had substantial prior data) in the absence of regulation.[2]

Nonetheless, public reporting in all three countries is unsystematic and idiosyncratic, which limits accountability. One of our main findings was that there is an urgent need for clear guidance on best-practice reporting categories and how to measure them, in order to enable meaningful comparisons to be made between companies. We note that regulation to report to government can help in this regard. Where it requires reporting on specific categories of workers (as in the US, for example) these categories can be used in public reports. For benchmarking purposes, CSR benchmarks, such as that run by Opportunity Now in the UK, provide similar guidance. We found a desire in both the UK and Australia for further reporting guidance, and in Australia this was considered necessary with regard to reporting to government, as well as reporting to the public. While the debate as to whether or not to regulate for public reporting on social and environmental issues continues, our study indicates several other important and complementary avenues for improving reporting practice. These are the focus of our recommendations, which are as follows.

Companies should routinely report gender-disaggregated HR data. Reporting their key HR performance indicators with gender breakdowns will have the effect of immediately increasing transparency on gender equality.

Our study has revealed a quite urgent need for standardised reporting KPIs. Governments and/or business organisations should consider producing best-practice guidance for corporate public reporting on workplace gender issues. This would best be developed in collaboration with civil society organisations. It needs to provide consistent, comparable reporting indicators and identify agreed ways of measuring these.

In Australia, the Equal Opportunities for Women in the Workplace Agency (EOWA) should consider helping to improve corporate accountability to the public by commenting on or evaluating company CSR reports on gender equality in the workplace.

Ways need to be found to increase the capacity of civil society organisations to inform companies better about their expectations on gender reporting and thereby to enhance their impact as stakeholders.[3] Both government and business could take initiatives in this regard.

Companies may need to anticipate some scepticism about those website reports, updates and newsflashes on gender workplace issues that are not clearly verifiable or audited. We recommend that stakeholders are invited to review and give feedback on gender reporting, and that this feedback is included as part of the external audit of the sustainability report.

CSR and sustainability reporting awards should extend to gender equality/diversity reporting. These could be sponsored by government agencies (such as Australia's EOWA), business organisations (such as 'Opportunity Now' a programme of Business in the Community in the UK), or accounting bodies and CSR organisations (eg ACCA).

2. Research has shown that large companies are more likely to report. Our sample consisted of the largest companies in each country, however the Australian companies were on average considerably smaller than the UK and the US companies in our sample. This may partly explain the fact that Australian companies in our sample reported less information, and also suggests that regulation to report to government, or to the public, may have a greater impact on small companies than large ones.

3. For a discussion of gender equality and stakeholder relations please see Grosser (forthcoming).

1. Introduction

This report addresses three related and pressing questions.

- To what extent do large companies report publicly on equal opportunity for women and gender issues[4] in the workplace?

- How has private sector reporting of these issues developed over the last decade in the UK (the country for which we had substantial prior data)?

- What influence has the trend of corporate social responsibility had on this reporting?

These questions are addressed by examining how companies reported issues of gender equality in the workplace in three countries that reflect different regulatory environments for such reporting – Australia, the UK and the US. Following a content analysis of published reports, both paper and web-based, interviews were conducted with company representatives in two of the three countries, Australia and the UK, in order to:

- investigate the drivers of reporting

- clarify the processes that shape the content of reports

- illuminate the prospects for improved reporting.

This introduction continues by outlining the aims of the research and revisiting the findings of previous literature on the subject. We then discuss our methodology, summarise the context of reporting in the three countries, and introduce the developments in CSR in the last decade, and their potential effects on reporting. We note the limitations of the study and set out the structure of this report.

1.1 AIMS OF THE RESEARCH

The aims of the research were to investigate:

- the extent and nature of reporting on women's employment issues in a sample of the largest companies in Australia, the UK and the US

- the extent to which disclosure on this issue has improved in the UK (the country for which we had substantial prior data)

- the impact of regulatory and voluntary approaches to equal opportunities reporting

- the extent to which and the ways in which CSR has become a driver of corporate social disclosure (CSD) on gender equality in the workplace.

4. Gender issues in the workplace are referred to in a variety of ways in the literature and in company reports. The discussion is framed in terms of equal opportunities for women, gender, gender equality and gender diversity. We use these terms interchangeably to mean gender equality in the workplace unless otherwise stated. Gender equality is often addressed as part of a broader diversity agenda.

1.2 LITERATURE REVIEW

In this review, we look first at empirical studies of how companies have reported women's employment issues, and at the recommendations that those studies have made; we then briefly examine the theoretical frameworks that have been used to explain why companies report (or not).

Much of the earlier research on corporate accountability for equal opportunities has been conducted in the UK where reporting on women's employment issues is voluntary.

Adams et al. (1995) study reporting by the top 100 UK companies for the reporting year ending in 1991. The study examines disclosures in annual reports on: specific equal opportunities policies; other evidence of equal opportunities commitment; and reference to external pressures, initiatives and legislation. While 82% of organisations reported an equal opportunities policy on applications/ recruitment, and 62% on training, only 48% reported that they had policies on promotion/career development for women.

There is no legal requirement in the UK to disclose information on women's employment; however, there is legislation with respect to the employment of disabled people. Given our interest in the relative effects of voluntary and regulatory approaches, it is worth noting that Adams et al. find that only 34 companies complied fully with this legislation in the corporate annual report, 52 complied partially, while 14 made no mention of disabled employees (Adams et al. 1995). These findings suggest that legislation that requires disclosure to the public but that is not enforced is not fully effective and that other mechanisms, in particular social regulation, may be required to ensure public accountability.

Adams and Harte (1998) and Adams and McPhail (2004) study reporting on the employment of women (from 1935 to 1993) and ethnic minorities (1935 to 1998) respectively, in annual reports in the UK banking and retail sectors. They chart the impact of the changing social, political and economic contexts on corporate (non) disclosure. They show how corporate reporting has not only been used to influence societal views about women's and ethnic minority employment, but also how it reflects changing social, political and economic contexts.

Adams and Harte (1999) report on the portrayal of equal opportunities performance in three organisations in the UK from a variety of stakeholder perspectives.[5] They find that detailed performance data collected for internal

5. The stakeholders included: trade unions representing the workers in the three organisations; the Equal Opportunities Commission (EOC); the Commission for Racial Equality (CRE); and two organisations which monitor the ethical and social performance of organisations – the Ethical Consumer Research Association (ECRA) and the Ethical Investment Research Service (EIRIS). Adams and Harte (1999) also included examples from academic literature; a database search for legal cases; and had contact with the industrial tribunal offices in Scotland and England.

purposes (eg to monitor compliance with equal opportunities legislation in the event of an Equal Opportunities Commission (EOC) or Commission for Racial Equality (CRE) investigation or a court case) were not reported or summarised in the external company reports included in their study. This suggests that the collection of data required for reporting to government agencies in Australia and the US will not necessarily lead to its use in public reporting.

Adams and Harte (2000) make five proposals for firms to improve accountability and transparency for equal opportunities and discrimination. Firms should:

- publish details of equal opportunities policies

- report on their achievement of policies

- report quantified equal opportunities targets and their monitoring results

- publish details of equal opportunities investigations conducted, and complaints made, in respect of their equal opportunities performance

- introduce equal opportunities information systems with the assistance of workers and statutory equal opportunities organisations.

Adams and Harte (1999) conclude that the various self-regulatory initiatives (eg contract compliance, mutual regulation through commercial contracts, voluntary self-regulation, a 'good equal opportunities employer' logo for high-performing companies) would have a limited impact on accountability. Despite their reservations about regulations that require minimum reporting to the public, they conclude that this is the approach most likely to improve accountability. It should be stressed here that regulation in Australia and the US requires only limited reporting to government; there is no requirement to report to the public.

In 2001 the Kingsmill Review of Women's Employment and Pay in the UK notes that:

> The driver of the virtuous circle in which business incentives prompt a strategy to promote diversity, which in turn deliver greater profits, is information. This means information and quantitative data available at the firm level to generate both an understanding of where best practice lies, and a situation in which those firms which are getting their human capital management right are rewarded through higher levels of investor confidence and ultimately high shareholder value. (Kingsmill 2001: 51)

In the US the Glass Ceiling Commission (US Glass Ceiling Commission 1995: 15) stated that 'Public disclosure of diversity data – specifically, data on the most senior positions – is an effective incentive to develop and maintain innovative, effective programs to break glass ceiling barriers', and recommended 'that both the public and private sectors work toward increased public disclosure of diversity data'. It argued that in addition 'The government should also explore the possibility of mandating public release of EEO-1 forms for Federal contractors and publicly-traded corporations'. Ten years later a study by SRI investors (SIRAN 2005: 3) endorsed the call for greater disclosure of diversity data, arguing that 'Without adequate EEO disclosure, SIRAN analysts are not able to assess certain risks and opportunities associated with existing or potential investments'. They found public disclosure of EEO data by US companies continued to be unsatisfactory, and urged government to reconsider mandatory disclosure.

More recently, Calvert (2008: 14) found that EEO disclosure by US companies had decreased since 2005 and reasserted its belief that 'corporate disclosure of diversity demographics data, such as EEO-1 data, is critical to understanding and addressing the effectiveness of diversity initiatives, as these data identify the extent to which women and minorities are moving up the corporate ladder'. It concludes that 'Greater disclosure is essential to further progress on diversity, as in virtually every other social, environmental, and governance issue that Calvert addresses, and will benefit not only interested stakeholders, but also the companies themselves'. It recommends increased detailed disclosure of corporate diversity practices.

Finally, Grosser and Moon (2008) analyse reporting on equal opportunity for women by 20 leading UK employers who prioritise gender equality in the workplace, and who rate themselves highly in terms of their external communication on this issue.[6] The authors examine annual reports, CSR reports and company websites. Whereas earlier studies find that equal opportunity reporting is mostly in terms of policy, Grosser and Moon (2008) find significant reporting of performance information on gender in workforce profiles, and some performance reporting on women's recruitment and career development. There was also some reporting of litigation (2 out of 20 companies), and reporting on several other key gender issues, such as equal pay (8 out of 20 companies). Nonetheless, they note the unsystematic nature of this reporting, which makes comparisons between organisations difficult.

Grosser and Moon (2008) interviewed HR, diversity and CSR managers and found business support for government plays a role in developing guidance for reporting on gender/diversity. Such guidance, they suggest, might include reporting of gender disaggregated data, and reporting on gender equality issues of importance to civil society (eg equal pay, job segregation, flexible working). They suggest reporting compliance with the Equal Pay Act (1970) and the Sex Discrimination Act (1975), reporting Opportunity Now impact benchmarking results, and reporting of company stakeholder engagement on gender issues. They recommend that government support and enhance market drivers for better

---

6. These were employers who benchmark their progress with Opportunity Now, the UK Business in the Community gender equality programme.

disclosure through public procurement contracts, and provide capacity-building for civil society organisations working in this field to enable them to participate more fully in reporting processes.

Our present study similarly investigates the reporting of performance information, analysing annual reports, CSR reports and company websites (see Adams and Frost (2004) on the use of the Internet for CSD). In this study, however, we examine such reporting in the largest companies in three countries.

There have been few comparative studies of reporting on gender equality and other equal opportunities. Gray et al. (1987) compare a study of social reporting by US companies (Ernst and Ernst 1978) with a study of financial reporting by 300 British firms (Tonkin and Skerrat 1983). They find that US companies reported on the employment and advancement of women much more extensively than companies in the UK (Gray et al. 1987: 60).

Theories about CSD
A number of theories have been developed to explain CSD and, in particular (non) disclosure on women's employment issues. These are outlined in Adams et al. (1995), who conclude that legitimacy theory[7] cannot explain the instances of (non) disclosure; in particular, the lack of compliance with legislation that requires reporting on disabled employees in the corporate annual report. Adams et al. (1995) conclude that the results of their study were more consistent with the political economy framework, used in Tinker and Neimark's (1987) analysis of the portrayal of women in the annual reports of General Motors between 1917 and 1976.[8] Tinker and Neimark (1987) conclude that annual reports were used as ideological weapons rather than as reports of 'the facts', as the nature of women's exploitation changes with the crises facing capitalism.

This view is criticised by Cooper and Puxty (1996: 299) both for underplaying the social context and for failing to allow women to 'speak for themselves'. Their view is supported by Adams and Harte's (1998) and Adams and McPhail's (2004) evidence of how changing notions of patriarchy and attitudes to race influence the reporting on women and ethnic minority employment respectively. Adams and Harte (1998: 808) conclude: 'A *history* of employment in banking and retail, drawing on the

corporate annual reports when set in the social, political and economic contexts can be seen to be largely *his* story' [emphasis in original].

Stakeholder theory has also been used to explain CSD as a way to communicate with stakeholders and manage stakeholder relations (eg Gray et al. 1996). CSR is often explained in terms of stakeholder relations (eg Freeman 1984; Freeman et al. 2007). Grosser and Moon (2008) conceptualise the influence of CSR on CSD in terms of the way different stakeholder groups are reinforcing each other within new systems of governance such that we are witnessing a 'socialising of markets', including on gender issues (see sections 1.5 and 1.6).

In summary, previous empirical research in the UK finds CSD on equal opportunities for women to have been unsystematic, varying across individual organisations, sectors and time, and, until recently, limited to policy and programme reporting with very little information about outcomes and performance. A number of key influences are identified, including: the Second World War; unemployment levels; equal opportunities legislation; pressure from the CRE, EOC and trade unions; government rhetoric; the changing nature of work; patriarchal views; demographic changes; and CSR.

The contribution of the present study
This study builds on previous research by examining the nature and extent of reporting on equal opportunities issues for women in three countries: Australia, the UK and the US. This enables, first, comparison of disclosure patterns in these different regulatory contexts and, secondly, evaluation of the effects of recent developments in CSR. We note the gender content of the relevant national and international CSR and socially responsible investment (SRI) benchmarks and indexes (Grosser and Moon 2005) that may have had an impact on disclosure. Our comparative research into CSD on the reporting of gender equality in the workplace adds to the literature by revealing the extent to which new forces for greater gender equality have affected disclosure.

Adams (2002) argues that the development of theory about CSD has been limited by the lack of any explicit attempt to engage with those companies which do report – particularly regarding the impact on external reports of their internal processes of reporting and the attitudes of managers to reporting. She found that these were two important factors determining the nature of disclosures and the level of accountability discharged. Grosser and Moon's interviews (2008) with UK managers found that increased internal monitoring and CSR have encouraged greater disclosure on gender issues by UK companies. They also found that a lack of pressure from civil society organisations working on gender issues helped to explain a lack of external reporting of the data collected internally.

Accordingly, the present study uses interviews with managers from the companies in the sample to identify the internal processes and motivations for reporting on gender equality.

---

7. Legitimacy theory, as later defined by Adams and Harte (1999), assumes that firms will seek to portray themselves in a socially acceptable manner and to legitimise their business actions through disclosures.

8. The political economy approach to accounting is 'concerned with exploring and assessing the ways various social protagonists use accounting information and corporate reporting to mediate, suppress, mystify and transform social conflict. The approach places class relations at the forefront of the analysis and is, accordingly, concerned with the effects of accounting information and corporate reporting on the distribution of income, wealth, and power' (Tinker and Neimark 1987: 71–2).

1.3 METHODS

Our sample consisted of 24 companies, eight from each country. These included the largest four companies overall from each country, and the largest two banks and retail companies in Australia,[9] the UK and the US.[10] We included banks and retail firms because they are leading employers of women and to provide continuity with previous studies of CSD in the UK (Adams and Harte 1998, 1999).

The research consisted first of content analysis of corporate annual reports and CSR reports for the year ending between 1 February 2005 and 31 January 2006, and of company websites from February to June 2006. We looked for reporting on 25 issues relating to gender equality, covering: workplace profile, equal opportunity at work, work–life balance, litigation, and management accountability for gender equality/diversity. As we found no reporting on two issues[11] our analysis is of the remaining 23 issues (see Table 1.1). Company reporting on gender equality beyond these categories is covered in section 2.5 under 'Reporting on other gender workplace issues'[12] and in section 2.7 and Appendix 1 on reporting of awards and benchmarks.

For each of the 23 issues we had four categories of data for the reporting of:

* performance
* targets
* action
* policy information

making 92 data categories altogether. General or aspirational targets were excluded, (eg unsubstantiated statements that the company wanted to increase women in management).

---

9. Our Australian sample consisted of four banks, two retail companies and two others. This was because the largest companies in Australia included more than two banks.

10. Our selection was based on the Forbes Global 2000 list of February 2006. We measured size by turnover as comparable data on number of employees were not available.

11. These were: information about women part-time workers by grade, and the take-up of flexible working options by gender. The fact that there was no reporting on these issues is significant because women make up the majority of part-time workers, and the progress of these women to higher levels of the workforce affects the gender pay gap. The take-up of flexible working options by gender is an important indicator of the extent to which organisations normalise such working practices. In the UK, the Chair of the EOC has concluded that: 'While some employers were improving attitudes to flexible working, they tended not to apply the same principles to very senior jobs' (Jenny Watson, Chair of the EOC. See Teather 2006).

12. Further minor references to gender, by one company only, have been omitted for reasons of space.

Table 1.1: Items included in the reporting analysis

	Reporting on women's employment patterns
1	Women in total workforce
2	Women in management
3	Women at different grades/job categories
4	Part-time workers
5	Women as part-time workers
6	Women as casual workers
7	Women from ethnic minorities
8	Women from ethnic minorities at different grades/job categories

	Reporting on gender equality/diversity in the workplace, and how it is managed
9	Women's recruitment
10	Women's retention
11	Women's training
12	Women's career development
13	Women's redundancy
14	Women in non-traditional jobs
15	Work–life balance (including parental leave and flexible working)
16	Childcare
17	Equal pay
18	Equality and diversity training
19	Employee opinion surveys on gender/diversity group
20	Results of employee opinion surveys by gender/diversity group
21	Litigation relating to gender/diversity
22	Sexual harassment
23	Gender and diversity in management appraisal

Our analysis focuses on performance reporting because this is particularly important in enabling stakeholders to evaluate the policies and action/programmes that companies report. We examine the reporting of trend data because some managers consider them to be key indicators of performance (Grosser and Moon 2008). We include reporting about gender, and diversity more generally (when it appeared to include gender), equal opportunities, and work–life balance.[13] In addition, we examine reporting of overall governance structures associated with gender/diversity.

Our indicators were developed from those used by Adams et al. (1995), Adams and Harte (1998) and Grosser and Moon (2008) and from priorities on gender as expressed by government, business and civil society organisations. We recorded the location of reporting of each issue, whether it was discursive or quantitative, and the time period and geographical coverage given.

Our interviews were conducted with CSR, human resources (HR) and diversity managers in six Australian and six British companies. These focused on:

- the reasons for monitoring and reporting on gender equality, including:

  - the role of legislation

  - the role of external reporting guidelines and CSR benchmarks

  - the role of market actors

  - the role of civil society organisations

  - stakeholder feedback

  - explanations for reporting deficits

  - views on reporting of bad news

  - views on future reporting frameworks

- the processes of reporting, such as:

  - determination of target audiences and reporting content

  - use of external reporting guidelines

  - processes for stakeholder feedback

  - organisational participants involved

  - internal use of data.

The two main limitations of the study are the small size of the sample, which means that findings are indicative rather than statistically representative of wider reporting practice, and that interviews were not conducted with US companies.

1.4 THE REGULATORY CONTEXT IN AUSTRALIA, THE UK AND THE US

Both Australia and the US have regulations requiring companies to report certain information about gender equality in the workplace to government, whereas in the UK there is no such mandatory reporting of employee data except regarding disabled people and, in Northern Ireland, religion. The UK Department of Trade and Industry (DTI) has, however, issued guidelines on human capital reporting that imply that best practice would include reporting on gender and diversity issues (DTI, 2003).

In addition to legislation, governments can use 'soft' regulation to facilitate, partner and endorse CSR on workforce diversity, including tax and public contract incentives, for example. In the UK this has included the government's *Accounting for People Report* (DTI 2003), childcare tax incentives, and the inclusion of diversity criteria in public authority procurement using new regulations designed to create a public sector duty to promote race, disability and gender equality. A new Equality Bill (Government Equalities Office 2008) extends these procurement initiatives. In the US and Australia reporting to government on gender is also linked to government procurement. A detailed analysis of business/government collaborations and partnerships on gender issues in the three countries is beyond the scope of this study. We have, however, summarised some of the main ways in which gender issues have been incorporated in to CSR inititiatives that affect business in these countries.

The UK organisations studied by Adams and Harte (1999) identified strong incentives for voluntary collection of data that, in Australia and the US, is legally required to be reported to government. One such incentive found in the UK study was the need to demonstrate compliance with equal opportunities legislation. The EOC had been actively involved in monitoring corporate equal opportunities practices through both 'collaborations' and official investigations; it also emphasised the importance of monitoring in its Code of Practice (EOC 1985; see Adams and Harte 1998). Companies prepared special reports, following 'collaborations' with the EOC, which were not made widely available. In addition, data on equal opportunity issues was demanded and carefully monitored by the relevant trade unions, as was company involvement in initiatives such as 'Opportunity 2000' (Adams and Harte, 1999).

Table 1.2 compares the regulatory frameworks in each country by the type of organisation (by size and function) required to report; the issues to be reported; and access to and presentation of, the information collected.

---

13. When the diversity reporting is specifically about other groups (eg ethnic minorities, older workers) it has been excluded.

Table 1.2: Regulatory differences regarding CSD on gender equality in the workforce in Australia, the US and the UK

Australia

Size of organisation required to report	**Type of organisation required to report**
>100 people.	private, public and others.

Issues organisations are required to report on	**Issues of data access/presentation**
Suggested: women and men by job category and type. Required: women by recruitment, promotion, transfer/termination, training and development, work organisation, conditions of service, sexual harassment, pregnancy and breastfeeding. Required to show staff consultation in this analysis; list priority issues, actions taken, evaluation, planned actions. Suggested minimum: 6 pages.	Reports are available for public access, except for salary information and evaluation of actions taken and their effectiveness – which may be kept confidential. These are substantial parts of the reports to Equal Opportunity for Women in the Workplace Agency (EOWA), and their lack of availability to the public has been cause for concern for unions. Companies can be waivered from reporting for three years after producing a particularly good report. Data is not available to the public during this period.

US

Size of organisation required to report	**Type of organisation required to report**
>100 people (and government contractors with more than 50 employees and contracts worth $50,000 or more).	Private companies.

Issues organisations are required to report on	**Issues of data access/presentation**
Numbers and percentage of gender and race in different job categories: (officials and managers, professionals, technicians, sales workers, office and clerical, craft workers, operatives, labourers, service workers). Gender and race cross-referenced.	Not available to the public. Government publishes some analysis of aggregate data.

UK

Not applicable

Table 1.2 shows that the size of companies covered by Australian and US regulation is similar, but Australian regulation requires descriptive analysis of the barriers facing women and action taken to address them. The US legislation requires disclosure to the government only, while in Australia it requires reporting to government which makes some of this information available for public scrutiny.

The lack of full disclosure in publicly available company reports on women's employment issues in Australia has been a subject of national debate. The Finance Sector Union (FSU) called for major banks to make public their full equal opportunity reports after three big banks were given 'female-friendly' Employer of Choice awards by the Equal Opportunities in the Workplace Agency (EOWA). The FSU stated: 'At a time when the finance sector has the worst gender pay gap of any industry (women earn just 57% of what men earn), our members are curious to know how these awards are judged' (Finance Sector Union 2005). The EOWA has since tightened the criteria for the Employer of Choice awards and increased transparency in this respect. In May 2007 it announced new criteria, which require organisations to have management consisting of at least 27% women, a gender pay-gap of less than the national average of 17%, and minimum maternity leave available, in addition to other requirements.[14] Lack of disclosure of equality data produced for government has been the subject of debate in the US also, and identified as a problem for investors there (SIRAN 2005)

While the regulatory context is important, in particular the US and Australian regulations to report to government, our conclusions in this report are informed by the fact that the public reporting we examined in corporate reports and websites is entirely voluntary and not directly governed by the legislation.

---

14. Organisations applying for the 'EOWA Employer of Choice for Women' citation are now required to demonstrate the following requirements in addition to the original criteria: equal opportunity for women is a standing agenda item on a committee chaired by the CEO or his/her direct report; female managers can work part-time; paid maternity leave – minimum of six weeks' paid leave after 12 months' service; sex-based harassment training is conducted at Induction for all staff (including management, contract staff and casual staff), and refresher education or update is received by all staff (including management, contract staff and casual staff) every two years; pay equity gap between average male and female salaries **at each level** of the organisation is less than the national gender gap identified by ABS research (currently 17%). Additionally, the organisation's **overall** pay gap must be less than the organisation's industry average pay gap, based on current ABS statistics. Both calculations are based on ordinary time earnings; at least 27% of managers are women or the number of female managers is greater than the industry sector average (EOWA 2008).

1.5 THE BLOSSOMING OF CORPORATE SOCIAL RESPONSIBILITY

Whereas previous literature has taken account of a wide range of social, economic and political influences of CSD, the present study considers one particularly relevant recent development. This is corporate social responsibility (CSR), which has arisen in the context of new systems of societal governance and new market conditions (Moon 2002, Moon and Vogel 2008, Vogel 2005). Changes in governance structures in society, and particularly the growing role of business in these, have raised new questions about business–society relations and the new focus on CSR has been one response to these. This has been a long-term theme in the US, though the UK is now regarded as the international leader (Vogel 2005) with Australia lagging behind (Australian Government Department for Environment and Heritage 2005; Batten and Birch 2005) but witnessing new enthusiasm for CSR (Birch 2002, Moon and Sochacki 1998). Most research into the reporting of gender workplace issues (see section 1.2) predates these developments.

Even the sceptics recognise significant developments in CSR. Clive Crook, Deputy Editor of *The Economist* observed that 'over the past 10 years or so, corporate social responsibility has blossomed as an idea, if not as a coherent practice' (*Economist* 2005: 13).

The growing profile of CSR is evident in its status within companies. Many have designated organisational responsibilities for CSR at both the managerial and board levels. Some companies have employed CSR managers who are responsible for developing and managing CSR policies and programmes. A CSR consultancy industry is mushrooming (MacCarthy and Moon forthcoming), indicating that companies are willing to pay for expertise in the area. An increase in CSR membership and non-profit organisations (eg Business in the Community [UK]; Business for Social Responsibility [US] and the more modest St James Ethics Centre [Australia]),[15] often associated with CSR standards, benchmarks and tools, also indicate growth.

Significantly for our research, CSR has been associated with a dramatic growth in company reporting of their social impacts and responsibilities, be it on their websites, in free-standing reports and within annual reports. In the last five years, over 90% of the FTSE 100 have issued some report of their CSR, however defined. This reflects the assumption that a responsible company is one that reports its activities. Australian companies report on CSR less frequently, with 23% of the S&P/ASX 100 reporting in 2005, compared with a 16-country average of 41%, and a UK average of 71% (Australian Government Department

---

15. Examples elsewhere include: The Copenhagen Centre (Denmark); the European Corporate Governance Institute; the CSR Europe Academy; the Institute for Social and Ethical AccountAbility, Jobs and Society (Sweden); Business and Society (Belgium); Hellenic Business Network for Corporate Social Responsibility (Greece); Fundacion Empresa y Sociedad (Spain).

for Environment and Heritage 2005). There are now international awards for socially responsible reporting, such as the annual ACCA Awards for Sustainability Reporting.

Why, then, is this trend taking place? The answer appears to be summed up in the phrase the 'socialisation of markets' (Moon 2003), which indicates that, although some companies explain their CSR in terms of their core values and others might reflect the values of certain corporate leaders, there is a strong sense in which CSR represents company responses to external pressures and influences. We can classify these as market, civil society and governmental.

Market influences

A number of market drivers have emerged which contribute to the growth of CSR: consumers, employees, investors, competitors, and business customers. These clearly affect companies in different ways, but we will consider them here in general terms.

One of the market drivers is new consumer demands. These should not be exaggerated, as the socially responsible consumption captured in opinion research is not supported by other evidence on spending habits. Nonetheless, there are clear niche markets of consumers who are prepared to pay more for goods and services that they consider socially responsible (eg cosmetics free from animal testing; organic foods; ethically sourced coffee and chocolate). Moreover, consumers can be mobilised to have greater mass impact, illustrated by the US boycotts in the 1990s of branded clothing sourced in Bangladesh and more recently in Burma. The importance that companies place on consumers' responses to their CSR policies is evidenced by company polling of consumers in order to evaluate their CSR.

Another contributing factor is that employees are increasingly regarded as a driver for CSR in three main respects. First, employers are being made aware that employees' job choices, particularly for graduates, are in part informed by the broader reputation of companies, including their CSR. Secondly, some employees are keen that the companies are involved in their immediate communities. Thirdly, certain employee demands, such as those concerning work–life balance, are increasingly met not simply through a company's HR policies but also through its CSR policies.

While the impact of socially responsible investors should not be exaggerated, two developments should be underlined. First, there is a small growth in dedicated socially responsible investment (SRI) funds, particularly in the US and the UK, but also in continental Europe. Secondly, mainstream investment funds and stock exchanges are increasingly giving attention to risk and governance factors, which many companies address in CSR terms. Many companies see CSR as part and parcel of their competitive edge, be it in response to any of the three factors mentioned above. This, in turn imposes pressures on their competitors to match their CSR investments (Porter and Kramer 2002).

Finally, for many small and medium-sized companies, and particularly those in global supply chains, business customers, especially in the branded retail markets, are imposing CSR standards through their supply chain assurance and audit systems.

Civil society influences

Although social drivers are often manifest through consumers, employees and investors, it is worth distinguishing collective social pressures that reflect changing social expectations of business:

- NGO influence
- media attention
- business associations/coalitions for CSR.

Some NGOs have acted adversarially to draw attention to the social irresponsibility of business (eg Christian Aid's critique of CSR), and this, or the anticipated effects of such action (sometimes referred to as social regulation), has come to inform CSR. Paradoxically, perhaps, this has sometimes led to NGOs (eg community organisations, international campaign groups) and companies or business associations entering into partnerships to encourage, develop, manage and report CSR (eg Oxfam, WWF, Amnesty International). More generally, companies are tending to enter into more long-term relationships with community organisations and charities in order to pursue their CSR programmes (Moon and Muthuri 2006). CSR has also emerged as a more pressing topic in business education and research (Aspen Institute 2008; Matten and Moon 2004).

The media have also acted as a driving force for CSR simply because of their appetite for stories about social irresponsibility, often through an implicit partnership with certain NGOs. There are also CSR media manifest in specialist journals and magazines (eg *Ethical Corporation* and *Ethical Performance* in the UK, and *The Corporate Citizen* in Australia); as well as electronic networks for CSR professionals (eg *CSR Chicks*, *CSR Blokes*, *Lifeworth*). Mainstream media have shown an increased interest in the topic, including regular CSR features (eg the *Financial Times* (UK), *The Age* (Australia)).

Governmental influences

Many governments have shown great interest in encouraging CSR (Moon and Vogel 2008). The UK government is a leader here, having a Minister for CSR and a variety of policies and initiatives to coax corporations to be more socially responsible.

At a most basic level, governments can endorse business social responsibility, as illustrated by former prime ministers Tony Blair (UK) and John Howard (Australia). Governments can facilitate CSR not only by the provision of organisational support for CSR events, but also with subsidies of CSR organisations and activities. This form of encouragement can also extend to more explicit partnerships (eg the UK's Ethical Trade Initiative for labour standards in supply chains from developing countries). Governments introduce 'soft regulation' to encourage more responsible business (eg the 1999 amendment to the UK Pensions Act requiring the reporting of social, environmental and ethical impacts). Finally, governments can encourage CSR by building certain issues into public procurement contracts, as discussed in section 1.4 above.

In the context of these developments, two recent reports in Australia included in their remit an examination of sustainability reporting (CCMAC 2006; PJCCFS 2006). In their submissions to both inquiries, the business and professional bodies generally viewed the current status of social and environmental reporting as adequate, whereas those organisations representing stakeholder groups were generally in favour of further moves to mandate CSR reporting (Adams and Frost 2004). Similar differences were reflected in UK debates over reporting of the Operating and Financial Review.

1.6 CSR AND GENDER REPORTING

The recent reporting of gender equality in the UK workplace has taken place in the context of a growing focus on CSR, which has led to rapid increases in corporate social disclosures or sustainability reporting (terms we use interchangeably[16]). Indeed Grosser and Moon (2008) found that companies were more likely to report information about gender and equality in their CSR reports and in CSR sections of their websites than in their annual reports. In the context of steady increases in women's labour market participation since the 1970s, and the growing importance of human capital management (eg CIPD 2005), companies focus more intensively on how to improve not only their human capital management but also their reputations with regard to gender and diversity. Increased costs incurred by litigation are also important (Henderson 2002). Another major factor is changes in technology, which has led to an explosion of web-based corporate social reporting.

Diversity and gender equality are increasingly defined as important CSR issues. Despite considerable limitations in the gender content of CSR and SRI benchmarking and reporting systems, gender is specifically included in some form in many key CSR initiatives (Grosser and Moon 2005). BITC has a specific gender equality programme (Opportunity Now), and gender equality in the workplace is included, for example, in the GRI reporting guidelines, in BITC's Corporate Responsibility Index, in the FTSE4Good and the Dow Jones Sustainability indexes; and non-discrimination is an issue which is covered in many CSR supply chain codes of conduct.[17] SRI investors have sometimes focused specifically on gender issues (eg Calvert 2004; Henderson 2002; SIRAN 2005, 2008). Table 1.3 illustrates some of the ways that gender equality has been included in CSR tools in Australia, the UK, the US and at the international level.

Our analysis investigates how these various forces help to shape the reporting of gender issues at the workplace.

---

16. We have used the term 'sustainability' because this is used by ACCA and by some companies when describing their reports. However, we also refer to 'corporate social responsibility' reports. Recent evidence shows that increasingly companies are using the terms corporate responsibility or corporate social responsibility in describing their reports, rather than sustainability (KPMG 2005). Leading academics have also raised the question as to whether sustainability is the most appropriate term for company reporting (Gray 2006).

17. Limitations in the way that gender equality is included in these CSR initiatives include: the limited scope of gender indicators; the fact that reporting on gender issues is often optional; and the fact that gender issues are often subsumed within the category 'diversity', and with reference to supply chain codes, women often work in informal supply chains not covered by such codes.

Table 1.3: Examples of CSR and CSD initiatives and gender benchmarking

Initiatives	Gender references
International	
Global Reporting Initiative	The Global Reporting Initiative has created a partnership with the International Finance Corporation (IFC) to improve corporate reporting on gender issues through the development of a *Gender Sustainability Reporting Resource Guide* (GRI 2008b).
GRI Financial Services Supplement (GRI 2002a)	Includes gender indicators. Includes equal pay.
The Global Compact	Principle 6 – elimination of discrimination.
OECD Guidelines for Multinational Enterprises (OECD 2000) and many other international codes of conduct for business	Includes non-discrimination on grounds of gender.
UK	
Opportunity Now (part of Business in the Community)	Employer-led gender in the workplace benchmarking, advice and awards. Approximately 180 firms.
BITC CR Index	Includes gender and diversity in the workplace criteria.
FTSE4Good	Includes gender criteria.
Female FTSE Index (academic and government-led)	Ranking of companies according to percentage of women on company boards.
Other gender-specific investor initiatives	eg *Socially Responsible Investment: Closing Britain's Gender Pay Gap* (Henderson Global Investors 2002).
UK's 50 Best Workplaces (Great Place to Work Institute UK 2008); and the *Sunday Times '100 Best Companies to Work for in the UK'* lists (Best Companies 2008)	Contains significant gender content.
Aurora's *Where Women Want to Work* website (Aurora 2008a) *The Times 'Where Women Want to Work Top 50'* (Aurora 2008b)	Business response to demand for information about companys' performance on gender equality. Includes transparency and reporting criteria.
The CSR Competency Framework (DTI 2004)	One of the Framework's six core characteristics is 'harnessing diversity'
WEConnect	UK supplier diversity initiative spearheading the connection of women-owned business and multinational corporations.
US	
Catalyst	Employer-led research and advisory organisation for advancing women in the workplace; awards.
Working Mothers magazine (Working Mother Media Inc 2008)	Rankings and awards.
DiversityInc and other market-based diversity listings	Public rankings of companies on various diversity issues, including gender. Also resources and careers services.
Major supplier diversity initiatives	eg Women's Business Enterprise National Council.
Dow Jones Sustainability Index	Includes gender criteria.
Calvert's Women's Principles (Calvert 2004)	Most comprehensive investor guidelines on gender equality. Includes monitoring and reporting.
Fortune '100 Best Companies to Work For' list (Cable News Network 2008)	Includes rankings lists on number of women, on-site childcare, work–life balance, and telecommuting.
Australia	
BITC Corporate Responsibility Index	Inclusion of gender and diversity criteria.
RepuTex indexes	Minimal requirements relating to discrimination.
Government provides guidance relating to all six steps listed in 1999 legislation to advance women in the workplace (see Table 1.2 on page 13), and administers gender-related EOWA Employer of Choice Award (EOWA 2008)	For the criteria see footnote 13 on page 14.

2. Data on gender equality/diversity

2.1 INTRODUCTION

In this chapter we summarise first the overall reporting patterns found, and discuss companies' reporting of women's employment patterns and workplace profile. We then present our analysis of how companies report workplace practices on gender equality/diversity. Finally, we examine the way that companies report on their governance and management of gender equality/diversity.

2.2 OVERALL RESULTS

With regard to location of reporting our findings are that:

- companies report much more information on gender equality/diversity in their sustainability/CSR reports than they do in their annual reports

- UK companies report more of this information in their annual reports than companies in the other two countries

- UK and US companies report more information on their websites, mostly under the label of CSR, than in their hard-copy reports

- Australian companies report more in their CSR hard-copy reports than on their websites. This is true both of their reporting on gender equality in general and their performance reporting in particular (See Tables 2.1 and 2.2).

Table 2.1: Percentage of total information reported by location of reporting

Location	Annual report	CSR report	Web	Other
Total reporting for all three countries	13.2	53.3	67.8	13.2
Australian reporting	12.3	70.0	46.9	2.3
UK reporting	20.2	48.6	74.6	13.9
US reporting	6.3	45.0	77.5	21.3

Notes: Total figures amount to over 100 because companies often report the same information in several different locations.
'Other' includes specific diversity annual reports and diversity reports.
Website reporting includes CSR websites and also recruitment and general website information.

Table 2.2: Percentage of performance information reported by location of reporting

Location	Annual report	CSR report	Web	Other
Total performance reporting	9.1	57.9	60.4	14.0
Australian performance reporting	4.8	81.0	33.3	54.8
UK performance reporting	13.6	55.9	71.2	11.9
US performance reporting	7.9	44.4	68.3	22.2

Notes: Total figures amount to over 100 because companies often report the same information in several different locations.
'Other' includes specific diversity annual reports and diversity reports.
Website reporting includes CSR websites and also recruitment and general website information.

With regard to reporting performance information, a significant finding from this research is that nearly all companies (22 out of 24) reported some performance information on gender equality in the workplace, and all but one of these reported some relevant quantified performance information (Table 2.3). Moreover, 18 of the 24 companies reported some quantified information that reveals performance trends.

Table 2.4 shows the amount of performance, target, action and policy data reported, as measured by the percentage of reporting in these four categories on all 23 issues, by the eight companies in each country. So, for example, with regard to performance data, each company could potentially report 23 items of data (performance information relating to each of the 23 issues). With eight companies in each country, there are 184 items of performance data that could be reported for each country. In fact, no company reports performance data on all 23 issues. Table 2.4 shows the percentage of actual reporting found in each category for each country.

Table 2.4 also shows the percentage of total reporting for each country. With 92 categories of data for each company (23 items × 4 categories for each), and eight companies in each country, there are 736 items of data that could be reported for each country. The bottom line of Table 2.4 shows the percentage of these items actually reported for each country.

Table 2.3: Number of companies reporting performance, target, action and policy information*

	No. disclosing	No. disclosing quantified info.	No. disclosing trends
Australia			
Performance	6	6	5
Target	2	2	
Action	8		
Policy	7		
UK			
Performance	8	7	7
Target	5	3	
Action	8		
Policy	8		
US			
Performance	8	8	6
Target	2	2	
Action	8		
Policy	8		
Total			
Performance	22	21	18
Target	9	7	
Action	24		
Policy	23		

*This includes reporting on any of the 23 issues covered in our analysis.

Table 2.5 presents more detail on the amount of performance data reported, again as measured by the percentage of performance reporting on all 23 issues by the eight companies in each country.

Tables 2.6, 2.7 and 2.8 (discussed in detail below) reveal the number of companies reporting performance data, by issue reported, including quantified information and performance trends. These data reveal that more companies are reporting performance information on gender equality since the studies undertaken by Adams and Harte (1998 and 1999), thus confirming and extending the UK findings of Grosser and Moon (2008).

Table 2.3 (page 19) indicates that six Australian, eight UK and eight US companies report some performance data. Of these, all but one of the UK companies disclose some quantified data; and all but one Australian, one UK and two US companies disclose some trend performance data.

In terms of the amount of performance information reported (Table 2.4), US companies report performance on approximately 34% of items on our reporting index, UK companies 32% and Australian companies only 23%. In terms of trend performance data, Table 2.5 shows that UK companies report this on 11.4% of items on our reporting index, US companies 8.7%, and Australian companies 5.9%. The low overall percentage of reporting of trend data (8.7%) reveals a considerable limitation in reporting practice.

Table 2.4: Amount of reporting (percentage of data reported on all 23 issues)*

| Reporting type | Countries | | | |
	Australia	UK	US	Combined
Performance	22.8	32.1	34.2	29.7
Target	2.7	6.0	2.2	3.6
Action	28.3	36.4	35.9	33.5
Policy	18.5	20.1	15.2	17.9
Total reporting*	18.1	23.6	21.9	21.2

* Percentage of total reporting = reporting of 23 issues x 4 data categories (policy, action, target, performance information) x 8 companies per country.

Table 2.5: Amount of performance data reported (percentage of data reported on all 23 issues)

| Performance measure | Countries | | | |
	Australia	UK	US	Combined
Performance	22.8	32.1	34.2	29.7
Performance quantitative	17.9	23.3	28.2	23.1
Performance quantitative with trends	5.9	11.4	8.7	8.7

Table 2.3 reveals that nine of our 24 companies (five UK, two Australian, two US) report some targets relating to gender equality in the workplace for which they can be held accountable. Of these all but two UK companies report these as quantified targets. The reasons for not reporting more targets are numerous, but one company explained this as follows.

> We have set policy objectives and our businesses around the world have identified how best to achieve them...we have group policy objectives, but do not set group-wide targets because of different local circumstances...Targets, where appropriate, are set at business level. (Aviva CSR Report 2006: 2, 5, hard copy)

All companies report action on gender equality in the workplace (Table 2.3). UK and US companies report action relating to approximately 36% of items on our reporting index, while Australian companies report action on approximately 28% of items (Table 2.4). All but one company reported specific polices on at least one of the issues that we searched for (Table 2.3).

To conclude, our overall findings suggest a low level of reporting on gender equality workplace issues, but almost all companies (22) report some performance information, however limited. We find a notable increase in reporting of performance on this issue in the UK (the only country for which we have comparable data). Overall, UK companies report slightly more on this issue than their Australian and US counterparts (Table 2.4). This suggests changes since Gray et al.'s finding (1987) that US companies reported significantly more information on the employment and advancement of women than UK companies did.[18] However, collectively, US companies do still report slightly more performance data on gender equality than their UK counterparts. The best Australian companies report as extensively on this issue as leading UK and US companies; but, collectively, Australian companies report the least.

2.3 REPORTING ON WOMEN'S EMPLOYMENT PATTERNS

Company reporting of performance data (including quantified and trend data, and targets) focuses on women in management more than on any other of the 23 issues we examined. The number of companies disclosing information on various aspects of women's employment patterns is shown in Table 2.6.

Overall workplace profile by gender
Quantified information on the percentage of women in the workforce was provided by six Australian, five UK and seven US companies. Trend data were provided by only one Australian, three UK and three US companies. Only one company (Australian) provided information on targets for women in the workforce, and then only for its operations in one country (South Africa).

Data on the percentage of women in the workforce most frequently related to the whole workforce. Some companies, however, provide analyses of women in their total workforce broken down into specific countries, regions, or business units (such information is sometimes given via country or business unit sustainability reports or websites). For example, BP reports this information for Alaska specifically. BHP Billiton (BHP) reports the percentage of full-time staff who are women in Africa, Australia, North America and South America, as well as in its corporate offices. Aviva reports two years of data on women's representation in the workforce for 22 business units in more than 15 countries. General Motors reports the gender profile by hourly and salaried employees in 2004 for its operations in the Asia Pacific region, and for Latin America, Africa and the Middle East. In the case of Europe and for North America, General Motors provides these data for two consecutive years.

Women as part-time workers
Women make up the majority of part-time workers, so the results here are significant. Information on the number of part-time workers employed (Table 2.6) was disclosed by six Australian companies, four UK and three US companies. Of these, all but two of the Australian companies disclosed quantified information. Trend data on this issue were disclosed by two Australian and three UK companies, while no US companies did so. Such data are hard to compare because definitions of part-time working vary by country. Table 2.6 shows that two UK companies reported the number or percentage of female part-time workers, including quantified data. None of the Australian or US companies reported this information. However, our data analysis also revealed that two US companies reported the percentage of women casual workers, whereas no companies in the other countries did so.

Women in management and at different grades/categories of employment
The number or percentage of women in management (Table 2.6) was reported by five Australian, eight UK and seven US companies. Of these, all but one UK company disclosed quantified information. Trend data on women in management were disclosed by three Australian, five UK and three US companies (Table 2.6).

On women's representation at different grades or work categories (including different levels of management), four Australian, seven UK and six US companies disclosed information. Of these, all but one UK company reported quantified information. Two Australian companies, four UK and two US companies reported this information with trend data (Table 2.6).

Companies define women in management in very different ways. While many provide no information about their reporting categories on this issue, some disclose the number of people in each management category. These categories vary considerably by firm and sector. For example, in the oil and gas sector, both BP and Shell report the percentage of women in senior management/ leadership and indicate the totals in these categories.

---

18. Proof of this would require further evidence from a larger statistically representative sample.

Table 2.6: Number of companies reporting performance information/data on women's employment patterns

	Australia			UK			US			Combined		
	No. disclosing	No. disclosing quantified info. (with trends)	No. disclosing targets	No. disclosing	No. disclosing quantified info. (with trends)	No. disclosing targets	No. disclosing	No. disclosing quantified info. (with trends)	No. disclosing targets	No. disclosing	No. disclosing quantified info. (with trends)	No. disclosing targets
Percentage of women in work force	6	6 (1)	1*	5	5 (3)	0	7	7 (3)	0	18	18 (7)	1
Part-time workers	6	4 (2)	0	4	4 (3)	0	3	3 (0)	0	13	11 (5)	0
Women part-time workers	0	0 (0)	0	2	2 (0)	0	0	0 (0)	0	2	2 (0)	0
Women in management	5	5 (3)	2	8	7 (5)	3	7	7 (3)	2	20	19 (11)	7
Women in different grades/work categories	4	4 (2)	0	7	6 (4)	2	6	6 (2)	0	17	16 (8)	2

Targets in this table include discursive and quantified targets.
*This target was for only one country (South Africa), and was related to compliance with the South African Employment Equity Act.

Another way to increase transparency and comparability is to report on the percentage of women at different salary levels. Shell Norway, for example, reports the percentage of women in the top salary level of two different leadership categories.[19] In the retail sector, Sainsbury's reports data on the percentage of women store managers, regional managers, and department directors, as well as their representation in middle and senior management.

In the absence of standardised systems for reporting such information, it remains hard to make reliable company comparisons. Our findings from company reporting, as well as from interviews, suggest that sector-specific comparisons and benchmarks may be easier to develop than comparisons between sectors. Benchmarking of companies against themselves in order to assess progress on women in management is possible for the 19 companies in our sample that report some form of relevant quantified performance data (Table 2.6). The potential for such benchmarking depends on the comprehensiveness of the performance data reported. Aviva's reporting stands out for its inclusion of performance information about women in management over the last two years in 21 different business units in more than 15 countries.

In reporting women's representation at different grades/categories (including different levels of management), some companies disclose significant amounts of data. For example, Shell's Sustainability Report (2005) includes information about women's representation at three different levels of management for five consecutive years and its website includes six years of data. Shell also reports its tracking of the percentage of women in less senior positions and states that this information is to be reviewed annually.

US companies are required by law to report to government on women's representation in nine different job categories, and some use this data to report externally (eg Wal-Mart, Citigroup, General Motors).

This illustrates that regulation can influence public reporting practice. The US government publishes aggregate data that can be used as a benchmark by companies. For example, Wal-Mart (2005: 5) reports that it 'exceeds the nationwide percentage for women in the Officials and Managers category, and exceeds both the nationwide and retail sector composite percentages for female Professionals'. Government publication of aggregate data has informed shareholder resolutions at Wal-Mart and Home Depot in 2006 calling for publication of company data. Wal-Mart responded to this request by publishing it's EEO-1 data (data submitted to government), partly, it seems, owing to three impending class action law suits on gender discrimination, one of which is defined as 'material', while Home Depot did not publish the data. General Motors, as well as reporting gender by nine

different job categories and for its overall workforce in the US, also reported salaried staff by gender and employment level for four different levels of the workforce in Europe for 2003 and 2004.[20]

Investors have shown an interest in being able to compare the percentage of women in the total workforce with the percentage of women in management, regarding this as an indicator of progress on gender equality in the workforce. Seventeen of our sample companies reported these data, with five Australian, five UK and seven US companies reporting in both categories.

The US law that requires reporting on women's representation in nine job categories also requires disclosure of their race. Two of our US companies reported the percentage of ethnic minority women in their workforce in nine job categories. No companies in either Australia or the UK reported such data. This indicates again that regulation to report to government can facilitate public reporting.

This concludes our analysis of reporting on women's employment patterns and workplace profile. We now turn to the analysis of reporting on other key gender equality/diversity workplace issues.

2.4 REPORTING ON GENDER EQUALITY/DIVERSITY PRACTICE IN THE WORKPLACE

Fewer companies reported performance on gender equity/diversity practice than reported workplace profile information. The 14 workplace issues listed in Tables 2.7 (page 24) and 2.8 (page 26) are the ones we found most information on. Table 2.7 shows performance and target reporting on these issues. Twelve of these were reported on by fewer than half the sample companies.

Many more companies reported action on these issues. (The discussion that follows comments on these in the order they appear in the tables.)

Table 2.7 (page 24) shows that performance information on work–life balance was reported by over half our sample (13 companies) – four Australian, four UK and five US companies. This included data on performance relating to parental leave and flexible working practices. Quantified information on this issue was reported by three Australian, two UK and two US companies, of which only one (Australian) company reported trend information. There was no reporting of targets on this issue but 22 companies (eight Australian, seven UK, seven US) reported action to encourage work–life balance (Table 2.8, page 26).

---

19. Norway is a special case since individual data on earnings is placed in the public domain.

20. Calvert (2008) has noted a recent decline in the public reporting of EEO-1 data by US companies.

Table 2.7: Number of companies reporting performance information on gender equality/diversity

	Australia			UK			US			Combined		
	No. disclosing	No. disclosing quantified info. (with trends)	No. disclosing targets	No. disclosing	No. disclosing quantified info. (with trends)	No. disclosing targets	No. disclosing	No. disclosing quantified info. (with trends)	No. disclosing targets	No. disclosing	No. disclosing quantified info. (with trends)	No. disclosing targets
Work–life balance	4	3 (1)	0	4	2 (0)	0	5	2 (0)	0	13	7 (1)	0
Equality and diversity training	2	1 (0)	0	5	2 (0)	1	4	3 (0)	0	11	6 (0)	1
Employee opinion surveys on gender equality/diversity	2	1 (1)	0	6	4 (1)	1	4	2 (1)	0	12	7 (3)	1
Results from employee opinion surveys by gender equality/diversity group	0	0 (0)	0	1	1 (0)	2	1	0 (0)	0	2	1 (0)	2
Recruitment of women	1	1 (0)	1	2	2 (0)	1	3	2 (1)	1	6	5 (1)	3
Retention of women	2	0 (0)	0	1	1 (1)	0	3	2 (2)	0	6	3 (3)	0
Career development for women	2	1 (0)	0	3	3 (1)	1	2	1 (0)	0	7	5 (1)	1
Training for women	2	2 (0)	0	1	0 (0)	0	2	2 (0)	0	5	4 (0)	0
Women in non-traditional jobs	1	0 (0)	0	1	0 (0)	0	3	2 (0)	0	5	2 (0)	0
Childcare provision	1	1 (1)	1	2	2 (1)	0	2	2 (1)	0	5	5 (3)	1
Equal pay for women	3	3 (0)	0	3	1 (0)	0	0	0 (0)	1	6	4 (0)	1
Litigation	0	0 (0)	0	1	0 (0)	0	2	2 (1)	0	3	2 (1)	0
Sexual harassment	1	1 (0)	0	1	1 (1)	0	1	1 (1)	0	3	3 (2)	0
Gender in management appraisal	0	0 (0)	0	2	0 (0)	0	2	2 (0)	0	4	2 (0)	0

Targets in this table include discursive and quantified targets.

Childcare is a closely related issue. Table 2.8 (page 26) shows that 13 companies reported action on childcare provision, but only five companies reported any related performance information. These all included quantified data, and one company from each country disclosed trend data on childcare provision (Table 2.7). Box 2.1 illustrates reporting on these issues.

Box 2.1: Examples of performance reporting on work–life balance and childcare

Westpac report

- The group-wide percentage of employee satisfaction with work–life balance in five consecutive years (and in three years for New Zealand and Pacific Banking).

- The percentage of respondents to its staff survey with caring responsibilities.

- The number of employees taking parental leave in five consecutive years (no breakdown by gender).

- The numbers of families and children using its childcare centres at seven different locations over a five-year period.

NAB report

- States that their programmes have 'delivered encouraging results with 74 per cent employee satisfaction with work–life balance'.

- The number of full-time/part-time transitions in three different countries.

HSBC report

- Resolution of a UK pay dispute with Amicus union with a three-year pay deal linked to increased flexibility in working hours.

Citigroup report

- The number of people using its search engine for assisting employees to find suitable childcare services in Mexico.

Shell report

- Day-care centres and childcare allowance costs for 2002 and 2003 in Brazil.

Equality and diversity training was reported by 20 companies (see Table 2.8), but only 11 companies reported performance data on this issue (see Table 2.7). Of these, one Australian, two UK and three US companies reported quantified performance data. Reporting included the percentage of the Management Committee who have had diversity training (Citigroup), the number of staff trained and the related increase in awareness of diversity issues (Ford UK), and specific feedback from staff about the impact of this training (Royal Bank of Scotland). Only one company (UK) reported targets for equality and diversity training (Table 2.7).

Employee opinion surveys are increasingly being used as a way of monitoring progress on gender and diversity in the workplace. Such surveys had been conducted by most of the companies in the sample – all eight UK, six Australian and four US companies. Only two Australian, six UK and four US companies reported their performance with respect to surveying employees on these issues (Table 2.7). Of these, one Australian, four UK and two US companies reported quantified performance information and only one from each country reported trend data. Only one (UK) company reported having a target on this issue. Twelve companies reported taking action to use employee surveys to gather information about gender and diversity (see Table 2.8).

Companies often monitor results from employee surveys by gender and diversity. The Royal Bank of Scotland (RBS) explained that this survey 'enables us to determine the needs and perspectives of different employee groups in areas such as performance management, training, communication and engagement'. Nonetheless, only two companies (one UK and one US) reported any results from employee opinion surveys by gender equality/diversity, with only the UK company reporting quantified information (Table 2.7). Thus gender differences in employee satisfaction, for example, are not routinely reported upon. Only two (UK) companies report targets on this issue, one of which (Tesco) reports that it aims to have 'No statistical difference by age, sex or ethnicity in answer to the staff Viewpoint survey question 'I look forward to coming to work'. Companies reported other communication channels with their workers on this issue (eg employee focus groups, intranet surveys, see Chapter 6).

Fewer companies reported performance information on other workplace issues. On women's recruitment, six companies in all reported performance information (see Table 2.7). Of these, one Australian, two UK and US companies respectively reported quantified information, and only one (US) company reported trend data. One company from each country reported having targets relating to women's recruitment, yet 14 companies reported action on women's recruitment (see Table 2.8).

Similarly, performance information on the retention of women was reported by only six companies. Of these, only one UK company and two US companies reported quantified data, all of which included trend information. While no companies reported targets, 15 (three Australian, five UK and seven US) reported taking action on women's retention (see Table 2.8). Reporting on the retention of women often included information about rates of return from maternity leave. Aviva, for example, reported maternity return rates in 22 business units in more than 15 countries.

On women's career development, seven companies reported performance information (see Table 2.7). Of these, five companies disclosed quantified information, of which only one (UK) company reported trend data. Targets on this issue were reported by only one (UK) company, yet action on women's career development was reported by 20 companies (see Table 2.8). One example of performance reporting on this issue comes from RBS, which discloses that: 'Women are now equally represented in all full-time promotions and account for 85% of all part-time promotions, including 87% of part-time senior management and executive promotions' (Royal Bank of Scotland 2005a: 9). It bears mentioning that the company reports that 92% of its part-time workers are women. No companies reported performance data on gender equality in redundancy.

Only five companies in all reported any performance information about training by gender (see Table 2.7). All but the one UK company disclosed quantitative information, but none gave trend information. None reported targets relating to training of women but 12 reported taking action on women's training (see Table 2.8).

Table 2.8: Number of companies reporting action on gender, equality/diversity

	Australia	UK	US	Combined
Work–life balance	8	7	7	22
Equality and diversity training	6	7	7	20
Employee opinion surveys on gender/diversity	1	7	4	12
Results from employee opinion survey by gender/diversity group.	0	1	0	1
Recruitment of women	3	5	6	14
Retention of women	3	5	7	15
Career development for women	6	6	8	20
Training for women	3	5	4	12 ·
Women in non-traditional jobs	3	2	7	12
Childcare provision	4	5	4	13
Equal pay for women	1	4	0	5
Litigation	0	1	0	1
Sexual harassment	4	3	4	11
Gender in management appraisal	4	4	4	12

There was little reporting of performance information on women's employment in non-traditional jobs with only two US firms disclosing quantitative data (see Table 2.7, page 24). No trends or targets were reported, but 12 companies reported taking action on this issue (see Table 2.8).

We found disclosure of performance information on equal pay by three Australian and three UK companies, but none from the US (see Table 2.7). All three of the Australian companies reported quantitative data, whereas only one UK company did so. Five of the six companies disclosing performance information on equal pay were banks that employ high numbers of women, have high pay gaps and face increasing litigation over equal pay (see below). In the UK this issue has been addressed by investors (Henderson 2002). Equal pay has also been included in the financial services sector supplement of the Global Reporting Initiative[21] (GRI 2002a), which has informed reporting on this issue by some Australian banks (Chapter 3, page 33).[22] One Australian and four UK companies reported taking action on equal pay (see Table 2.8). None of the US companies reported taking such action, but one reported having a target relating to pay equity (see Table 2.7).

Reporting on equal pay sometimes included reference to bonus systems and part-time workers. Box 2.2 gives examples of equal pay reporting.

Box 2.2: Examples of reporting on equal pay performance and action

National Australia Bank report

- Comparison of average male and female salaries in senior management, management or pre-management categories in three different countries.

Westpac report

- Male to female ratios of fixed pay and total cash for five different levels of the workforce (non-management, junior, middle, senior and top management).

ANZ report

- Male and female salary differentials for four categories of workers (executives, senior managers, managers, and non-managers) and overall weighted average.

- An annual audit in pay equity and remuneration in Australia.

RBS report

- Rigorous checks are in place to compare male/female bonuses for full time/part-time employees at different levels of seniority and across different ethnic backgrounds. Any discrepancies are rectified.

HSBC report

- Its comprehensive equal pay analysis of senior executives in Brazil, France, Hong Kong, Mexico, the US and the UK.

- Finds no systematic gender bias and no difference in the base salaries offered to men and women although specific organisational levels and different countries show discrepancies.

- Its Group Chief Executive has stressed to all business heads the urgent need to identify and address any specific cases of gender pay inequality.

---

21. The Global Reporting Initiative (GRI) is a worldwide, multi-stakeholder network. Business, civil society, labour, investors, accountants and others all collaborate through consensus-seeking approaches to create and continuously improve the GRI *Reporting Framework* (GRI 2008) and *Guidelines* (GRI 2006). The latter provides guidance for organisations to use as the basis for disclosure about their sustainability performance, and provides stakeholders with a comparable framework in which to understand disclosed information.

22. Equal pay is now included in the new 'G3' GRI *Guidelines* (GRI 2006), but was introduced earlier in the GRI financial services sector supplement (GRI 2002a).

Only one UK and two US companies reported litigation on gender equality/diversity issues (Table 2.7, page 24). Only the US firms reported quantified data on this issue, and one of these included trend information. General Motors reports on discrimination charges giving three consecutive years of data, though the nature of the charges is not specified. Wal-Mart (2006: 42–4) reports on litigation, including details of three law suits relating to gender discrimination in which the company is a defendant. In one case, Wal-Mart reports that 'the resulting liability could be material to the Company' and for all three that it 'cannot estimate the possible loss or range of loss which may arise from this litigation'.

These findings are significant because a failure to report on litigation has been noted as a limitation in corporate reporting on equal opportunities (eg Adams and Harte 1999). Grosser and Moon (2008) found that this situation had begun to change in the UK. There were no targets reported on this issue, but one (UK) company reported action relating to litigation (Table 2.8, page 26). Related reporting includes that from General Electric (2006), which does not cover litigation, but provides information about employee concerns reported to the company Ombudsperson over five years, revealing that by far the largest number of concerns were about fair employment practices.

A closely related issue is reporting about sexual harassment. Performance information on sexual harassment cases was reported by one Australian, one UK and one US company, all of which disclosed quantified data (Table 2.7). Only the UK and US companies reported trend data on this issue. Four Australian, three UK and four US companies reported taking action relating to harassment (see Table 2.8).

Finally, a key issue for gender equality in the workplace is the extent to which managers are held accountable for progress on gender and diversity. We found performance reporting on this issue by two UK and two US companies (see Table 2.7). Only the US companies reported quantified data, but four companies in each country reported taking action on this issue (see Table 2.8). There is very little information from any company about the actual goals set for leaders in relation to diversity. Box 2.3 illustrates reporting on this issue.

Box 2.3: Examples of reporting on gender and diversity in management appraisal

Citigroup report

- 2005 was the third consecutive year its senior managers developed diversity plans and reviewed their progress with the Board of Directors.

- These are reviewed quarterly with performance linked to compensation.

- 3,000 of its top managers have diversity appraisals, including senior business managers, HR directors and managers of country offices.

Wal-Mart report

- The company announced in 2004 that it would tie diversity goals to executive compensation. Specifically, if company officers do not meet their individual diversity goals, bonuses are reduced up to 15%.

- Diversity goal requirements apply to 3,500 officers and senior managers, and 51,000 facility level managers.

- All officers achieved their diversity goals in the current year.

BP report

- Its leadership development programmes now include 'inclusion' using a feedback tool incorporating two questions on inclusive leadership behaviour.

- Accountability measures are rigorous and transparent. Performance contracts rate executives on behaviours (including on D&I) and business results and these ratings directly affect bonus and pay.

- All D&I targets are tracked quarterly; if goals are not met leadership intervenes.

Shell report

- Publishes its Diversity and Inclusiveness Standard, which requires that every Shell company includes diversity and inclusiveness performance in leaders' and employees' appraisal and development plans.

- The Standard is linked to the Group D&I Framework, which states that leaders are accountable for achievement of goals.

We found some reporting of poor performance or 'bad news' (beyond litigation and harassment) by two Australian, four UK and three US companies. Our interviews revealed that companies believe that such inclusions can enhance the credibility of their reporting (see Chapter 3). Box 2.4 illustrates reporting of bad news.

The process of annual reporting on gender/diversity systematically, the use of a company-wide template or key performance indicators (KPIs), and the habit of reporting against targets, can all increase the likelihood of reporting of bad news. For example, Aviva reports from 22 business units against the Group KPIs, which include women in management, and maternity return rates. Not all these data are positive but the information is still included in external reports relating to these business units.

The main issues covered in the reporting of policies were: recruitment, sexual harassment and career development, followed by training, work–life balance and equal pay. We also found a small number of policies relating to retention, redundancy, child care, and equality in assignments and transfers. Companies, especially in the US, sometimes reported that equality policies apply not only to employees and potential employees, but also to contractors, customers and service providers. They also sometimes reported compliance with existing equal opportunities laws.

2.5 REPORTING ON OTHER GENDER WORKPLACE ISSUES

We found reporting beyond the 23 issues in our analysis, such as on gender and age, especially in Australia (Box 2.5, page 30). The contemporary focus on the implications of an ageing workforce may lead to more reporting of gender aspects of this issue.

Some companies cover gender issues in their health and safety reporting. Citigroup details provision of lactation facilities and of breast cancer screening for a small number of women. Sainsbury (2005: 56) notes that 'a new stress policy has recently been issued building on the existing flexible working and fair treatment policies within the business'. Flexible working and work–life balance are included in Aviva's health and safety reporting.

Several companies comment on the number of women on their board.[23] Sainsbury's reports its joint Number 1 ranking in the UK Female FTSE Index and that women's representation in senior management and on the board was one of the company's frequently asked questions. Shell (2005a) reports its ranking in the Female FTSE Index for three years.[24] HSBC reports that the Board representation of three females is: 'more than most of the world's leading companies' (HBSC 2005). Ford (2005) reports having more minority or female board-appointed officers than any other company in the automotive industry, and Wal-Mart (2005) reports that its 14-member Board includes two females.

Finally, a number of US companies report on all diversity categories collectively (eg the percentage of officers who are women and ethnic/US minorities). Although such data can be useful, they do not enable discrimination by gender to be identified.

Box 2.4: Examples of reporting bad news

Westpac report

- A decline in employee satisfaction with work–life balance over four years, but a rise again in the most recent, fifth year.

Jaguar (a Ford business) report

- A small number of staff believe that they are being held back because of their ethnicity or gender.

Citigroup report

- Results of a staff survey feedback reveal that employees believe that their work schedules do not allow enough flexibility.

HSBC report

- No increase in the proportion of women in its 'talent pool' despite a recent commitment to achieve this, along with a continued commitment to focus on this issue.

---

23. As most company governance reports include the number of women on the board, this was not included in our study.

24. This is included in its reporting on the website of Aurora Gender Capital Management (Aurora 2008a) to which there is a link from the Shell website.

2.6 REPORTING ON GOVERNANCE AND MANAGEMENT OF GENDER/ DIVERSITY

We have noted company reporting on the inclusion of gender/diversity in management appraisal systems and female board-level representation. Drawing on our analysis of descriptive company reporting on these issues, we note that leading companies report an overview of their governance and management systems or structures to ensure that equal opportunity, inclusion, meritocracy, or diversity are advanced within the business. This includes reporting on such issues as:

- the diversity strategy and its main components
- lines of responsibility
- information about membership of key diversity committees, how often these meet, and to whom they report
- other internal monitoring and reporting procedures, such as the number of times a year that each business unit must report internally
- internal grievance procedures
- the incorporation of gender/diversity into business codes of conduct that are monitored throughout the business.

Box 2.5: Examples of reporting of gender and age data

NAB report

- Workforce representation of six age groups with gender breakdowns and the average ages of their Australian male and female workers.

Westpac report

- Group-wide breakdowns by gender in five age categories for five consecutive years.

- Gender breakdowns for these categories for three consecutive years in New Zealand.

- Acknowledgement of the barriers to work for women of mature age.

Woolworths (Australia) report

- Senior executives under 35 years old, including gender breakdown.

- The percentage of women in this group assessed as having potential for promotion.

Citigroup report

- The majority of its women employees are under 45 and 40% can be expected to have children.

We found that reporting refers to board or CEO commitment and sometimes includes statements from these sources. Companies that do not report an overall management structure on this issue will often report a board-level diversity champion. Others report that they have a board corporate responsibility or sustainability committee where equity in employment or diversity has been defined as a key CSR issue. Some companies, particularly in the US (eg Ford), report on how diversity is being integrated beyond HR and through the production chain. While leading UK companies also act to integrate diversity in their businesses (Opportunity Now 2004) they do not appear yet to report much about this. Sometimes these governance issues are included in the annual report. Such governance reporting has been described by managers as attempting to create confidence that the issue is being addressed effectively and is under control (Grosser and Moon 2008).

One example of such reporting comes from Shell's *Annual Report* (Shell 2005b), which provides one of the most comprehensive accounts of diversity governance. The 'Report of the Directors' in the *Annual Report* states the company's long-standing commitment to the integration of diversity and inclusiveness into every aspect of its operations and culture, through explicit expectations of all employees and leaders, underpinned by clear plans and targets. Its global diversity objectives, which include improving the representation of women in senior leadership to a minimum of 20%, and improving the positive perceptions of inclusiveness in the workplace, are also set out in the *Annual Report*.

As part of its sustainability reporting, Shell publishes its 'Diversity and Inclusiveness (D&I) Standard', which requires every Shell business to have a diversity and inclusion commitment, framework for action and assurance process, and to develop plans, goals and targets for improvement, as well as ways to measure, appraise and report business performance on this issue. An accompanying 'Group D&I Framework' outlines the requirements of leadership: to be accountable for achieving goals and results; to allocate adequate resources in each business to support the D&I plans; and to incorporate these objectives into key HR processes such as talent reviews. Progress must be monitored, measured and communicated quarterly to all employees in business units, and the company commits to external communication as well. The role of the business unit, D&I councils or forums in assuring progress on diversity is described. In addition, reporting reveals that all companies and joint ventures where Shell has operational control must apply the company's 'General Business Principles', including these on social standards such as D&I.

Citigroup (2005b: 5) incorporates a statement from its CEO about diversity management in its public reporting. This gives an overview of how the company has been embedding the principles of diversity and inclusion. It assures good governance on these issues by explaining that 'The Citigroup Diversity Operating Council, formed in 2000, is comprised of senior diversity and human resources leaders from core businesses and regions. It meets bi-weekly to review progress against our strategy, share best practices, and align policies globally'. It reports that 'in 2005 we continued to promote diversity globally through 24 business diversity councils, in which business leadership and employees from various levels and functional groups develop and execute initiatives'. It explains that these councils, each championed by a senior executive, are fundamental to the successful implementation of its gender and diversity strategy, and that they have objectives relating to talent, workforce development and work environment. It reports that all lines of business have diversity plans, and that progress against these is reviewed quarterly.

General Motors (2005) reports in its *Corporate Responsibility Report* that it has a Vice President, Corporate Responsibility and Diversity, whose team manages diversity, and that the issue is reviewed by the Public Policy Committee of the board of directors. Its diversity initiatives are reported not only to cover HR issues, but also to extend beyond these to cover other stakeholders. It reports having: strategic champions, responsible for integration and alignment across all major interfaces (consumers, dealers, employees, communities and suppliers); diversity partners (ie volunteers across GM who act as change agents and points of contact for information and resources); and affinity groups and councils, each with a senior leadership liaison, which together have over 3,000 members providing a formal link between employee groups and diversity, HR and senior management. These facilitate recruitment, retention and development of employees, and also support related marketing and product development.

Ford's reporting stands out for addressing diversity issues as they relate to its whole value chain (ie different stages of the production process). It reports (Ford 2005: 5) having an Executive Council on Diversity since 1995, and '10 employee resource groups, partnerships, local diversity councils and programs to promote flexibility and work–life integration'. It reports the Executive to be 'comprised of our president and chief operating officer, our group vice president for corporate human resources and labor affairs, and a top officer from each Ford operation'. Diversity is reported as relevant to eight out of nine of the stages in the company's value chain, including product planning and design, service, end of life, logistics, raw material extraction, parts and components, assembly and painting, and sales. While gender equality is not specifically identified in this discussion, it is reported as one of the 'broad sustainability challenges' which set the context for all the lifecycle stages in its production process.

The Royal Bank of Scotland is another company that includes these issues in its *Annual Report, Report of the Directors*: 'Each division has developed and delivered an action plan incorporating both Group and division-specific priorities to promote diversity across all areas of the employee lifecycle' (RBS 2005b: 113). It identifies ultimate responsibility in the appointment of its Executive Chairman of Retail Markets as the main board director accountable for the delivery of the Group's strategic diversity programme.

Aviva's CSR report (Aviva 2006) reports the launch of its diversity vision and strategy, the appointment of a group diversity director, and the establishment of a steering group made up of eight of the most senior directors around the world and chaired by a member of the executive committee. It is also one of the companies that publishes the terms of reference of such a steering group, in this case covering data gathering (customers and employees); enabling (employee networks and communications); integration (awareness, skills and embedding diversity in HR); and external impact on customers and investors.

Other companies have chosen to report on management or governance of diversity in different ways. Tesco's website (Tesco 2005) reported that the board asked the Diversity Advisory Group to analyse the diversity of the Tesco UK workforce compared with the UK population, and report results and actions arising from this analysis. BHP acknowledges human rights as 'basic standards of treatment to which all people are entitled, regardless of nationality, gender, race, economic status or religion' and that 'While human rights principles were originally intended to limit government action towards individuals or groups, many relate directly or indirectly to private sector actions' (BHP Billiton 2005b). It reports that it requires all sites to assess their sustainability and human rights risks and issues and to produce their own sustainability reports covering relevant local and regional issues.

Reporting sometimes includes details of stakeholder engagement on gender/diversity (eg Westpac 2005; Wal-Mart 2005), and how diversity has been included in the verification and auditing of company reports. This may be indicative of future directions in reporting practice. We include information about these issues as part of our discussion of reporting processes below (Chapter 6).

2.7 REPORTING OF AWARDS AND BENCHMARKS

Companies report their performance in winning gender or diversity awards and achieving high ratings in gender or diversity benchmarks. Sometimes they report the number of such awards achieved as well as the relevant award titles. For example, Ford reports that 'We have received more than 200 awards over five years from publications and organizations that recognize the value we place on diversity' (Ford 2005). Companies also validate the seriousness of their efforts and achievements by reference to participation in, and sometimes rank in CSR benchmarks (see Appendix 2).

2.8 SUMMARY

To sum up, we have found some detailed and extensive performance reporting on gender equality in the workplace in all three countries, as well as much reporting on programmes of action to address this issue. We find it is possible to benchmark many companies' progress on a number of gender issues which they have chosen to prioritise (eg women's representation in management). In this respect our findings show considerable progress from UK data a decade ago, reflecting findings of Grosser and Moon (2008).[25] In practice, the lack of comparable reporting systems and KPIs mean that opportunities for meaningful comparisons and benchmarking between companies are limited. This is an issue which was raised by our interviewees (Chapter 5). In addition the low overall percentage of reporting of trend data reveals a considerable limitation in performance reporting practice.

We find most performance reporting on gender equality covers women's employment patterns, but there is little reporting on women's representation in the part-time workforce. Performance reporting is much more limited in relation to key workplace issues such as recruitment, retention, and career development and training. Reporting is not confined solely to good news stories but includes some bad news. Nonetheless, we also find that accountability is limited for some of the issues which are most valued by civil society and government, such as equal pay, where there is no reporting on this issue in the US, and little overall reporting on litigation, sexual harassment cases and women's representation in non-traditional jobs. These findings are similar to those of Grosser and Moon (2008) suggesting that these trends in reporting practice are not isolated cases.

Our comparative analysis suggests that regulation to report to government is not a necessary and sufficient condition for better CSD to the public on gender equality, although our data suggest that it can facilitate such reporting, as seen in the use of government reporting categories in public reports by US companies. UK and US companies collectively report more information on gender equality/diversity than their Australian counterparts. This seems to be because fewer Australian companies report on these issues. Those that do so, however, report as extensively as UK and US companies, and in some cases are pioneering best practice (eg combined reporting of gender and age data). We have also found that US companies no longer report significantly more than UK companies on the employment and advancement of women (Gray et al. 1987). In the next chapter we examine the main drivers of company reporting on this issue.

---

25. Further studies using larger samples would help to ascertain the extent to which our findings are representative of general progress in reporting on gender equality performance.

3. Why companies take action on gender equality

We begin by looking at how companies justify focusing time and resources on advancing gender equality and diversity in the workplace, including monitoring and internal reporting of gender/diversity data.

Chapter 4 will look at why companies report externally on gender issues, and Chapter 5 explores the reasons companies give for not reporting to the public more of the data available internally. We discuss these findings in terms of market, civil society and government drivers. Chapter 6 also addresses these themes, but focuses on the processes behind reporting gender issues.

The reasons companies give for taking action on gender and diversity may be divided into the following areas:

- recognition of the importance of intangible assets, including human capital management

- reputation, brand management and increased stakeholder interest in gender and diversity issues

- monitoring, once in place, drives further action

- regulation to report to government

- values and the emergence of CSR.

We discuss these in turn.

3.1 THE IMPORTANCE OF INTANGIBLE ASSETS, INCLUDING HUMAN CAPITAL MANAGEMENT

Wanting to be regarded as an employer of choice motivates action on equality and diversity, particularly in the context of democratic change and increased participation of women in the labour market. The chairman's section in Westpac's *Annual Report* (2005) explains its focus on being a preferred employer in the context of the increasing importance of intangible assets.

70% of Westpac's market value is made up of intangible assets – things like the value of our customer relationships, our employee loyalty and commitment, and our governance and risk management capabilities. Our challenge is to demonstrate to the market the full value of these intangibles and to encourage the adoption of new metrics to more accurately capture our sustainable value...we are seeing initiatives to develop extended performance management accounts that attempt to capture this intangible value...For example, we provide indicators of how well we are leading our people for now and the future and how engaged they are in helping our customers achieve their financial aspirations. Recruiting and training our people costs tens of millions of dollars a year. So being a preferred employer and having relatively low employee turnover is an important driver of increased earnings and sustainability. (Westpac 2005: 3–4)

The chairman also explained that being a preferred employer meant that the commitment of their people 'flows directly into customer satisfaction and loyalty, and hence into earnings quality' (Westpac 2005: 7). Commitment is measured and found to be 'at an all time high of 69%, and in line with global best practice'.

Several companies specify the role of equality and diversity in the development of human talent. The BP group chief executive says: '...that is reflected in our policies of inclusion and meritocracy and determination to develop individuals, regardless of their background, creed or colour' (BP 2005a). General Electric (2005: 11) contends that companies with long-term success are 'energized by inclusiveness and a connection with people, which builds loyalty and commitment'. Thus various elements of the business case for gender/diversity (eg Opportunity Now 2001) are found in company reports. RBS's 2004 *Corporate Responsibility Report* reports on gender and diversity as well as its new award-winning Human Capital Model, which assesses the company's capacity to attract employees and secure their continuing commitment. General Motors (GM) highlights the centrality of diversity in its human capital management strategy, in the context of diversity of the global workplace, for a successful employee enthusiasm strategy. It therefore has a:

commitment to cultivate diversity by creating and maintaining a workplace environment that naturally enables every team member to make the greatest contribution. This requires a workplace environment that is free of discrimination, hostility and physical or verbal harassment with respect to race, gender, color, national origin, religion, age, disability, sexual orientation... (General Motors 2005)

This company reports that diversity can help 'to leverage differences as a competitive advantage for better problem-solving, more innovation and creativity, better products and services and, ultimately, meeting customer needs'. Thus the strategy to integrate diversity though all aspects of the business is explained in terms of brand management, employer of choice status and overall organisational effectiveness.

Some firms, such as Aviva, specifically refer to diversity as enriching the pool of talent and improving their understanding of their customers. Other companies focus on the benefits of work–life balance. BHP Billiton (2005a) describes these in terms of:

- increased productivity

- improved employee morale

- heightened employee commitment

- increased ability to attract and recruit the best employees

- increased workforce diversity

- improved health and safety record owing to fewer work-related incidents/accidents

- reductions in tardiness and absenteeism

- decreased turnover and, as a result increased return on training and development investments

- enhanced image and public relations.

Companies in all three countries report participation in government-led programmes to enhance workplace diversity or work–life balance, for example: Tesco participates in the DTI Work–life Balance Challenge Fund; ANZ in a government inquiry into balancing work and family life; and Ford Purchasing hosted a multi-company diversity forum, to encourage collaboration between business and government on diversity and work–life balance.

These examples reveal corporate action on gender and diversity stemming from an increasing recognition of the importance of intangible assets. Being an employer of choice is seen as a component of human capital management, and equity, diversity and work–life balance are described as increasing workforce attraction and loyalty.

Interviewees referred to the 'war for talent' for recruiting skilled staff, and ensuring that internal talent is fully utilised and retained. We found that companies regarded women's concentration at the lower levels of the workforce as not changing fast enough, so that their talent was not being maximised.

One of the main drivers is the view that if we don't have more significant representation of women in terms of actually being in the organisation and being in certain jobs and at certain levels, then we're missing out on a really significant part of the market for talent, and that's a problem and it's going to be a self-perpetuating problem because the more it occurs the more people will look at our figures and say – well women in particular will look and say – well why should I go there?...They're not delivering. (Bank, Australia)

Employees: recruitment and retention
Many companies referred to problems with women's recruitment and retention as a driver of action on work–life balance in particular.

Our retention rates are quite poor at the moment so that is another issue linked with gender. We're actually not getting the recruitment in numbers that we'd like...and we are also not retaining, so it all links back to these flexible policies...we're really at base one at the moment...and we're actually running a pilot...on parental leave retention, to...work through what the issues are. These are senior professional women where there's obviously been a lot of retention issues in the past...And typical things that come out, it's all based around our work–life policies. People, managers, [are] just not being flexible...we keep coming back to the same common denominators, so we know what the issues are, we've just got to try and fix them. (Bank, Australia)

Women's retention was recognised as inseparable from both their promotion within the organisation, and their access to part-time work at higher levels.

The real issue is around flexibility, and particularly for the women around flexibility in terms of hours...it's really looked at in terms of a lever to be able to retain more women at all levels and it should therefore flow through to more senior [levels]. (Retail, Australia)

Organisational culture
These issues were discussed in terms of having an inclusive organisational culture.

There are a whole range of other things that determine whether [people] stay or go...and a lot of that's around your culture and a lot of that's around flexibility, a lot of it's around the management, their leadership [on these issues]. (Australia)

It was widely recognised that improving the situation for women required changing the culture of the organisation and that this challenge is driving programmes such as greater consultation of staff, and job restructuring.

A great place to work means different things for different people. And to become more inclusive, we need to understand what those differences are and we need to remove barriers for people. So if a woman for example, [wants] to be a store manager, but actually a store manager is seen as being a full-time role, long hours, unsociable hours and they've...got a young child at home, we need to work on removing those barriers, and [understand] what is it that that individual needs and what can we do as a business to support that. (Retail, UK)

Leadership and commitment to shifting the culture of the organisation on the part of senior managers and the CEO were pinpointed as powerful drivers of action.

Eighteen months ago...we really were coming from a compliance focus. [Now] we've progressed in our approach...to a broader holistic view.. [What made the company shift was]...the survey from our team members and in particular from the senior leadership team, and...also...predominantly the commitment from the CEO. (Retail, Australia)

The desire to change the culture was also articulated in terms of the business need to have diversity of thought.

It is a competitive issue. One of the things that's...being spoken about is that diversity will give you thought diversity which is important if you want new ideas and innovation, and therefore how you grow your pool of talent is very much connected to diversity. So there's some links in there [in terms of] who you can attract and retain. And for [us] retaining women in senior positions has been an issue and I think if you look at the industry it's got issues there, it's a very blokey industry. (Bank, Australia)

Cost savings

Cost-savings were mentioned by many interviewees, relating in particular to parental leave and maternity return rates: 'if we can lift that up 10% the pay-off to the business has to be extraordinary'. This interviewee said that they ask managers: 'if you do lose that woman, what might that cost the business?' Another mentioned the benefits of developing your own talent rather than buying it in.

Labour shortages

Many interviewees specifically identified the ageing workforce and projected shortages in labour as the reasons for these issues grow in importance in the future.

Traditionally if a part-time employee has left it hasn't been perceived as the end of the world because we've got people that want to work in our business and we still obviously have that, but it's really around looking forward and trying to see potential difficulties that could limit or constrain business growth and address them early. So [when we talk about] the whole talent and workforce planning component...the gender and talent issue is wrapped up as part of that as a business issue. (Retail, Australia)

Investors

Whereas several interviewees perceived a growing interest in socially responsible investment (SRI) generally, some did not detect investor interest in gender and diversity.

I was taking care of Socially Responsible Investors relations and they were asking health questions, they were asking environmental questions, they were asking questions on the community investments, supply chain... [but] diversity and inclusion, it's never come up. (Oil and Gas, UK)

Nonetheless, interviewees from other sectors described how investors are beginning to value gender and diversity as human capital management issues.

We're beginning to see it [gender and diversity] referred to as [a] human capital value driver...and that's coming very much out of the war for talents, skills shortages, ageing population, demographics and all those sorts of issues converging...SRI [investors] have been doing this for a while but I'm talking about the mainstream markets. I heard someone from one of the unions the other day talking about the fact that in the last 12 months they've heard more [investment] analysts using the words human capital than they have in the last 20 years in their experience in the financial services sector. So I think we are definitely beginning to see a shift in thinking around [this]...the issue around human capital is increasingly becoming the main avenue in which financial analysts are engaging properly on factoring in externalities in the overall evaluation of companies...and diversity is one of the key ways to understand this because it's a way of increasing the amount of people you can recruit,... non-traditional recruitment channels...expand your skills base of potential employees, which is obviously going to become increasingly important in the next 10 years. So I

think the linkage is that this started in one area, became part of the business strategy, [and] is now beginning to be appropriately valued by the markets, so it's all kind of feeding back into itself. (Bank, Australia)

3.2 REPUTATION, BRAND MANAGEMENT AND INCREASED STAKEHOLDER INTEREST IN GENDER AND DIVERSITY

Increased interest in these issues by investors and employees as well as customers has meant that gender/diversity has grown in importance as a reputation and brand management issue. Our interviewees described the benefits of reflecting the customer base, as well as issues of attracting and retaining employees and appealing to socially responsible investors, as related reasons to take action. A number of interviewees talked of the variety of stakeholders who they believe are now interested in gender equality and diversity, such that the legacy of poor employment practice that some were aware of within their organisations was no longer tenable.

Gender diversity, specifically, is at the top of the agenda as far as I'm concerned. That's not because the other strands of diversity are not important, it's a simple reflection of the fact that we have to improve the most in this area. As an organisation we've been around for [a long time] and our senior management make-up in terms of male/female gender mix here is not as good as we want it to be. You know, you could argue we're simply living with the legacy of our recruitment practices over the last 15–20 years but the fact is if we do nothing and just let things ride themselves out, we'll probably have to wait another 20. So it's clearly not good enough... from our perspective but also [from] the perspective of all our stakeholders, whether that's shareholders, investors, employees...it's the full mix of stakeholders...whose issues that we have to address. (Bank, UK)

It is not only market actors that are acknowledged. Several interviewees referred to the way civil society organisations – such as NGOs and community organisations, the media, and unions – can influence business reputation and brand (see also section 3.5 on values and CSR).

Community in general does have a view about all this stuff because the media completely paint a picture for people and that's why being a family-friendly or a women-friendly employer is quite an easy thing for you to look at in terms of it being a differentiating factor between [us and the other] three major big banks. So from an attraction perspective it's something you can easily focus on that will make a difference for you in terms of your brand. (Bank, Australia)

These findings reflect the 'socialisation of markets' we find within the field of CSR (as described in section 1.5, page 14, and also section 3.5 on page 37).

3.3 MONITORING

As noted by Kingsmill (2001) monitoring and internal reporting can act as crucial drivers of company action on these key gender/diversity human capital issues: 'We know it's a problem but until you see it in stats, in black and white, that's when [managers say] 'Oh yeah, you're right', and start addressing the problem rather than just talking about it'. One interviewee said that since the company had '...started measuring performance around these issues [they] are now suddenly waking up to the fact that they can drive organisational improvements on the basis of these types of non-financial performance indicators'. Another explained how:

> Internal data probably has been the most compelling driver for our shift...[There were] two sets of really strong data...one was internal survey feedback showing that diversity wasn't strongly valued...and people felt we could do more from a work–life perspective, and also [monitoring showed] that [in terms of] women in senior management...we still remain a very traditionally male-dominated organisation...(Retail, Australia)

One interviewee said that collecting detailed data had led to the decision to develop a diversity strategy with a diversity project team and advisory board. Interviewees explained the vital role of monitoring in enabling management to be accountable for their progress on gender equality and diversity, which has been crucial in the process of change. Increased internal reporting helps to drive progress when senior managers, and managers in other parts of the business, can see the data from each business unit. This has the effect of creating internal competition between business units and accelerating progress on gender equality in the organisation. We analyse these monitoring and reporting processes in Chapter 6 (see page 48).

Systematic internal monitoring and internal reporting critically influences external reporting (discussed in detail in the next chapter). A number of interviewees in both the UK and Australia told us that their monitoring systems still limit their ability to report, especially when data are still collated manually. However, other companies had developed sophisticated monitoring systems. Monitoring is driven by both mandatory and voluntary initiatives.

3.4 REGULATION TO REPORT TO GOVERNMENT

Interviewees from several Australian companies mentioned government regulation on monitoring and reporting gender equality in the workplace as a driver of action.

> From a change management point of view I think [EOWA has] been quite critical because within the organisation we've got a number of people that have been with us for a long period of time...[with] quite entrenched ways of doing things....But...there's sort of a growing awareness... of how closely the gender issue is linked to managing, maximising talent and the effectiveness of the organisation to address needs... diversity issues and that sort of thing. So...the external reporting mechanism has helped us to really crystallise where we're at and...provide more internal focus on some of these issues...and discuss...[whether] we are progressing fast enough... It's been very helpful... just to have that discipline around the requirement for external reporting and reporting into the centre so that we can pull that together... we make sure that copies [of the EOWA report] go back to the HR teams for all areas of our business. (Retail, Australia)

The regulation to report to government in Australia has made a significant contribution, with respect to monitoring in particular.

> Well I think broadly the legislation's played a really important role because...we have to collect data in order to meet the compliance requirements from the Australian government,...we've done that and it's certainly helped us, and the [EOWA] report's taken really seriously here... [The] CEO [has to sign it off] and he takes great interest in what that data is telling us. So if that legislation wasn't there I'm not sure we'd go into as much depth in the data collection, [which]...forms a really strong platform for... analysis. (Retail, Australia)

The annual requirement to report has ensured that monitoring is systematic and consistent. This Australian interviewee said that if the legislation disappeared tomorrow the company would still collect the data because of their value, given the company's 'integration of diversity into everything we do'.

Another Australian company considered that the EOWA, and the monitoring that it required, had helped them recognise 'that these issues are actually important to our employees and to the performance of the company'. Access to EOWA data, which suggests that business performance can be enhanced through improving gender equality, and the opportunity to benchmark against EOWA data, are also considered important contributions of government regulation in Australia.

Interviewees in another Australian company said that, because they had been developing gender equality programmes for many years before the EOWA regulation, the legislation had not influenced their approach. It was the previously inactive companies that seemed to have benefited most from the regulation.[26]

3.5 VALUES AND THE EMERGENCE OF CSR

The issues described in section 3.2 above reveal the influence of market drivers on the way that companies address gender and diversity issues. Some interviewees specifically described this process in terms of CSR and sustainability. One commented on 'broader sustainability... and in particular the way that the external markets are increasingly valuing company performance on the basis of these sorts of issues'. She specifically referred to recent changes in employee attitudes.

We are finding graduates...have more exposure to a lot of the sustainability type issues...I think there are quite a few companies now that are...saying that they are finding graduates do consider it to be a point of differentiation in terms of choosing where they go [and particularly this is about] the culture, it's in how they treat their employees. (Bank, Australia)

Many interviewees described taking action on gender equality and diversity because it is the right thing, or the socially responsible thing to do (see also Adams et al. 1995). A number linked these ideas to notions of, and programmes for, CSR and increasing interest in the social and environmental impact of companies.

Several UK interviewees said that their membership of the CSR employer organisation Business in the Community (BITC) and its gender programme, Opportunity Now, has been central in driving their monitoring and action, particularly through the Opportunity Now gender equality benchmark and related advice service. Others mentioned CSR-related employment benchmarks such as *Great Place to Work* and *Best Place to Work* (both UK), and socially responsible investment benchmarks (eg the BITC corporate responsibility index) as helping to drive effective monitoring and increased action (see section 3.1 above on socially responsible investment and human capital management). Other employer organisations have also encouraged this process. For example, two interviewees indicated that the British Retail Consortium (BRC) had facilitated discussion among member companies about how best to monitor progress on gender and diversity.

Interviewees confirmed that gender and diversity are increasingly recognised as CSR issues: 'if you had to put a few key issues that CR should cover within an organisation,

then I would have thought that equality and diversity would have to be there'.

One interviewee summed up the impact of greater public interest in the social responsibility of companies on shifting the company from a compliance to a business strategy approach to equality and diversity.

When we looked at corporate responsibility as a key... strategy incorporated within our DNA, I don't know, the light switched on for people, or there was a shift in understanding [in terms of looking at] where does diversity fit into the business case, and why does it have such a major impact on the execution of our strategy...it's made a major difference to the culture and approach to diversity. (Bank, Australia)

The importance of these influences varies by country. An interesting cross-country comparison was made by one interviewee.

I do think that...[strategy is] better thought [through] in the UK and in Europe, in terms of [the] dynamics being much more [about] practical business. Whereas in the US it's more [about] equal rights like...black people, women...in Europe it's more about inclusion and how you can make sure that everybody in the business is feeling that they love what they do, they can bring their whole person into work and then we can have the best delivery of all, which is really the business case for Diversity and Inclusion...So I think the spirit [in the company] is European, even though we've been using a lot of the experience that our US colleagues have. (Oil and Gas, UK)

Another interviewee also referred to the relative UK progress on these issues.

The challenge I face in my role is to make sure that...our relatively good position [on gender] in the UK...is mirrored in the many other countries in which we operate, where it's certainly not as good.

As noted in section 1.5 on CSR, governments can play a role beyond the use of legislation. Many interviewees in both Australia and the UK described partnerships with government to identify best practice on gender, work–life balance, flexible working and equal pay among other issues. Nonetheless, one Australian interviewee believed that gender equality had declined in prominence as a public policy issue and that the government is not doing enough to address this issue.

There's not a lot of people banging on your door saying 'OK, if the government's not going to do this then big corporations should be getting this right'. The only one is the ACTU or the union movement saying...'OK the government's not changing policy on this, so we're going to now introduce it as part of negotiations or enterprise agreement deals to, say, private industries', OK you have to stand up. (Bank, Australia)

---

26. Previous research has established that large companies are more likely to report social and environmental information than smaller ones. Thus our focus on large companies may underestimate the impact of Australian regulation, which could have had greater impacts upon smaller companies that may previously not have been monitoring or reporting at all.

3.6 SUMMARY

The reasons companies give for taking action on gender/diversity issues are wide ranging and include:

- their recognition of the importance of intangible assets including improved human capital management

- their reputation and brand

- the results of monitoring and internal reporting enables and encourages further action

- regulation to report to government

- a response to increased awareness of values and the growth of CSR.

In section 3.1 and 3.2 above we noted increased interest in these issues from market and civil society stakeholders. For most companies a combination of all these factors drives concerted action. One interviewee said:

> *Well I think there were three drivers...The first is that gender diversity or diversity in general was a commercial reality, we have to reflect the markets in which we operate. Secondly, it's a socially responsible thing for us to be doing as an organisation, [and thirdly] to make sure that there is an equal playing field for all people and that we're actually reaching out to all potentially talented individuals within the organisation. (Bank, UK)*

4. Why companies report externally

In the previous chapter we looked at the reasons why companies take action on gender and diversity. In this chapter we investigate:

- why companies report externally on their actions to advance gender equality/diversity

- whom they regard as their main audiences

- what they hope to achieve by publicising these issues.

Our interviewees point out that various market stakeholders, especially employees and investors, are interested in information about company action in the areas of gender and diversity, reflecting our findings in Chapter 3. Thus, firms want to reflect emerging practice externally to enhance reputation and build trust: 'it would be silly to have a big diversity agenda [where] one of the focuses is women going on in the company and to have nothing about it in the public forum' (UK). They also report in order to benchmark their progress against other companies.

Reporting is driven by a combination of these factors.

I think first and foremost, it's stakeholder feedback, whether that's from formal mechanisms, such as the AGM, or whether that's through direct requests coming in from shareholders or investors [asking] 'what is your stance on this?' I think secondly...we don't want to see this as a bolt-on...extra activity and I think that's the same for the whole of diversity...I think thirdly it's driven by the need to he able to be easily benchmarked. (Bank, UK)

Investors and employees (both potential employees and current staff) were the two most commonly mentioned drivers, not only in regard to action (Chapter 3), but also to external reporting.

4.1 INVESTORS

SRI investors were seen as particularly important drivers of sustainability reporting. One interviewee described being asked about the number of women in senior management and on the board by SRI and mainstream investors. One described investor interest in their staff engagement programmes. Another explained that financial analysts were interested in the company's paid parental leave, because it had increased the company's retention rates. These cases had encouraged external reporting on these issues.

For investors...diversity...is about how well we manage our workforce and our talent and it's about being able to retain the best people so you get the job done. It's actually a signal to them of the quality of the management and leadership of the company. There [are] early signs that they're...starting to view the people information that way...so it's kind of a lead indicator...That will grow, and part of [this growth comes from] the education [of investors] about [what] these indicators signal. (Bank, Australia)

Individual shareholders also demand information about diversity which, one interviewee thought, informed the CEO's interest.

We've had questions about diversity in the AGMs...Also before the AGM we had to prepare [material to use] in case we got questions on this. So I think there's a general expectation that our shareholders are interested [in reporting]...We certainly had to prepare our corporate affairs team in terms of what are our diversity initiatives and some of the metrics we're looking at. (Retail, Australia)

Other interviewees expressed disappointment that investors did not read their CSR reports.

The issue of staff who are also shareholders was raised, in terms of their entitlement to information on HR, including gender and diversity.

4.2 EMPLOYEES AND POTENTIAL EMPLOYEES

Interviewees explained external reporting on gender equality in the workplace as lifting 'our profile as an employer of choice for women'. Several told us that information about gender equality and diversity is increasingly being requested during recruitment, leading some companies to disseminate CSR reports on the recruitment circuit.

One interviewee (Bank, Australia) said that having diversity programmes 'does play a big part in the perception of us being [an] employer of choice in a market where the skill shortage is becoming more profound'. This was confirmed by the fact that 'The recruitment firms we use continue to give us feedback about what potential candidates say about [the company] and why they want to come to us, so [we know our diversity work] is a real draw card' (Bank, Australia). These facts were given as reasons to report on the issues publicly. Reporting beyond the basic GRI indicators on gender/diversity was explained by some as an attempt to portray the firm's particular commitment to these issues, to potential recruits and to staff.

In some companies, the internal audience is described as a more important driver of company public reporting on gender and diversity than the external audience. One interviewee explained that:

[within the company] *people want to know...what percentage of* [workers] *are female and how does that break down throughout the levels...[and particularly]* in *your more senior positions.* (Bank, Australia)

Despite internal reporting to employees via the intranet:

The external report is probably the most concise source of information for [staff]*...[and therefore]* we want to make sure that we're reflecting the interests of all parties...investors, our end customers and also what the staff are saying. (Retail, UK)

The information needs of staff were given as a reason to report the entitlements of full-time as opposed to part-time employees by one interviewee, and as a reason to report on equal pay by another. One interviewee explained the reasons for detailed reporting in terms of taking the debates forward with working parents.

The numbers allow us to discuss the issues in a much more open and transparent and accountable manner. [For example] *we can talk about the issues we face with the provision of childcare services for our employees because we publish the numbers on how many people can access it and how many kids of* [company] *staff are in there.* (Bank, Australia)

Reporting on work–life balance was described as particularly significant for the internal and external audience.

We feel strongly about being a family-friendly employer, so childcare or...parental leave, or the focus on women and flexibility is something we choose to report on because we, one, strongly believe in it, two, we're very committed to it and we want to be transparent about the uptake and the impact it has within the work environment for women, and [thirdly] *sixty-five percent of our workforce is female so it's something we can put a nice story to and...demonstrat[e] the impact* [of]. (Bank, Australia)

Specific requests for more information on gender and diversity also come from recruitment staff. This can lead companies to post information on their websites as a resource for all.

There were a number of other reasons companies gave for their reporting on gender and diversity externally. These were concerned with:

- customers

- reporting by competitors

- the board

- the influence of reporting on internal progress

- civil society expectations

- government requirements and best practice

- CSR.

We discuss each of these briefly below.

4.3 CUSTOMERS

Reporting was also described as a way to reach customers. However, interviewees in the retail sector explained that, despite being their most important stakeholder, customers are not seen as a major audience for external reports. One explained that they consider diversity issues in their advertising campaigns.

4.4 REPORTING BY COMPETITORS

Several interviewees described competitor pressure to report.

[Amoung] *the competitors that...we deal with in the financial services world, also the big FTSE 100 companies, leading retailers...information* [on gender and diversity in the workplace] *is becoming increasingly available and transparent.* (Bank, UK)

if you've seen reports [by another company in same sector]*...their gender data...is really impressive and we plan to do something similar,* [and] *there's another report I've seen where I thought 'gee, that's really transparent and it's very clear', and even if the data's not that great, it just shows that the organisations care about this stuff.* (Retail, Australia)

One interviewee said that because competitors report on equal pay 'it would've looked a bit glaring if we hadn't'. Cross-sectoral comparisons can also drive progress. A retail sector interviewee, having noted that banks now report on equal pay said: 'I don't know whether we have enough data to do that yet...[but]...It would be insightful to have that data internally'.

Companies also compete to have the best reporting: 'I think there's a benchmark set by other organisations and we follow that, but we try to go even further.' Taking best practice from other sectors offers an opportunity to stand out among peers. Noting that few companies in her sector were doing a great deal on corporate responsibility compared with the banking sector, one interviewee explained: 'it's an opportunity for us, we really see that as an opportunity to get ahead, to take a leadership position'.

4.5 THE BOARD

The range of stakeholders interested in the issue has made gender/diversity a 'hot topic' which the boards consider worth reporting upon.

[We] *are committed to increasing the number of senior managers that are women...And there is a lot of activity taking place within* [the company] *to address that. So because it's such a hot topic I guess...the natural thing would be to put it in the report to say to people outside 'Look, we are committed to doing this...this is what we already do, and also this is what's coming next'. It's a hot topic, it's got commitment from the main Board. They're the ones that say what they want it in the report...It is* [good for our] *image and it shows their commitment to making something happen.* (Retail, UK)

4.6 THE INFLUENCE OF REPORTING ON INTERNAL PROGRESS

Some interviewees explained that they report externally primarily because it produces change internally.

It's more a way for [the] *company to pull its heads together* [and ask] *'What is our position on all those topics, what do we think? What do we do? What would we aspire to do?' and it's actually forcing us into action. (Oil and Gas, UK)*

Ultimately...the information is absolutely right for us to share publicly, but internally we also see it as a tool for driving progress and... challenging [people, allowing us to show that]...this is the reality...[and ask managers] what are you doing to improve? (Bank, UK)

This interviewee explained that reporting has 'created huge expectation internally', which helps to drive change.

External reporting can be particularly important with regard to workforce targets.

At the front of our report... we report on our targets each year and at the end of each section we set goals for the coming year, and actually having that in a printed document that is given to external stakeholders has had a huge impact on the organisation and on senior people taking responsibility, and following up their data sources, and tracking how they're going to make sure that they can reach those targets. So it acts as a real driver. (Bank, Australia)

External reporting can support gender and diversity programmes within the company. One interviewee explained that poor staff feedback on this issue had generated concern that 'we might have plateaued...and...producing a very public Corporate Responsibility Report puts it back on the agenda...and is...a key driver for people to actually implement strategies that will help us reach our targets'.

Another explained that, although external reporting content is simply lifted from internal reporting:

having a more senior sign off on the performance figures, having more public accountability around performance has definitely shored up a lot of initiatives which may or may not have been subject to review at some stage. [This has increased] confidence around the value of this kind of reporting for the organisation as a whole...The transparency and our ability to report [helped] instil a culture whereby this is [no longer] about being a fair and equitable company, this is actually about delivering on a sustainable business model to shareholders and the community. (Bank, Australia)

Even so, this interviewee added that while external reporting helps, it is not the primary driver of change within the organisation.

I think there's been a shift in terms of... strategic thinking about the value of this kind of reporting...if you're a services organisation and your shareholder satisfaction is based on how happy your customers are, and how happy your customers are is largely based on how happy your employees are, then suddenly diversity issues become a whole lot more pivotal to that end game about shareholder satisfaction, and I think the thinking around that has become much more sophisticated and the

organisation has gotten a lot better about pulling together all the different strands in terms of managing [this], and... externally reporting our performance in these traditionally non-financial areas has played a part in it, but is one part, not the driver of it...(Bank Australia)

4.7 CIVIL SOCIETY EXPECTATIONS

Companies put considerable effort, often through CSR departments, into determining what people want externally, and what they are expecting to be able to access. Interviewees saw the community, NGOs, unions and the media as drivers of reporting on gender/diversity.

Several interviewees, especially from the retail sector, referred to 'community expectations' and one explained:

I think there's generally a much stronger push to transparency... in line with what the community expects of us. So...I think...it would be right to have some data on how many women we have in executive positions and operational roles and turnover rates generally...We've done quite a lot of work with local communities in the past and we have an opportunity to share that with the broader community through CSR reporting. (Retail Australia)

One UK interviewee explained that the 'main audiences when we're reporting on gender, would be a number of NGOs'. When asked which, this person said:

I think the NCC [National Consumer Council], and Which, and I suppose WI [Women's Institute], and there are lots of organisations like that who are very keen to see what our activity is in those areas. Not necessarily...to pass comment or to...pick us up on it, but just because it's a matter of interest. There's [also] an opinion-forming [community], there's an academic audience as well. (Retail, UK)

Nevertheless, no interviewees could give details of specific feedback or interest from NGOs on gender reporting, and one said that in her view NGOs do not read the company's sustainability report, despite being one of its primary target audiences.

Considerable media interest in CSR was noted, as was its role in reflecting and informing public interest and driving reporting, including on gender/diversity. This is because the press picks up specific stories, such as the appointment of a part-time female store manager, and then wants to flesh these out with data on women's position in the company.

Unions were noted as influences on external reporting on gender/diversity, including on flexible working which is growing in importance for them. Several interviewees revealed that they were discussing the content and frequency of their reporting on diversity and equal pay with their main union. Although communication with unions takes place via external as well as internal reporting, they still do not appear to be seen as a major audience for external sustainability reporting.

4.8 GOVERNMENT REQUIREMENTS AND BEST PRACTICE

In response to questions about the role of EOWA in Australian reporting, one interviewee from the banking sector said: 'we certainly wanted to make sure there was consistent reporting and, hopefully, [to share data between] both [government and CSR] reports'. However, the reporting period is not the same for these reports and, according to this interviewee, the information in the CSR report needs to be more precise and focused on what the company has achieved, rather than on what actions they have taken. Several interviewees believed that their approach to reporting on gender had been influenced a great deal by their reports to EOWA, and one suggested that they might try to get feedback from EOWA about their public report as well as their EOWA report.

Government is regarded as a driver of external reporting by pioneering best practice: 'probably the benchmark for diversity reporting is actually happening in the (Australian) government sector at the moment because… it's part of their compliance requirements'. A UK interviewee (banking sector) expressed the view that public sector organisations have sometimes led the way in reporting on gender and diversity in the workplace. UK legislation for a public sector duty to promote gender equality now requires public authorities to report on these issues.

4.9 CSR

Our interviews confirmed that CSR benchmarking and reporting has become a major driver of external reporting on gender/diversity. Our findings show that most reporting on these issues now takes place within sustainability or CSR reports and in CSR sections of company websites. Interviewees referred to increasing pressure to report on CSR issues generally 'to meet our requirements in terms of external reporting and comparison, and benchmarks to other organisations'.[27]

One said: 'I guess the message I would want to give is that [gender/diversity is] part of the CSR strategy, it is an absolute given in terms of our responsibilities and as an organisation' (Bank, UK). Another said: 'Even if people aren't asking us about it, part of being a responsible business is actually addressing some of these issues, not necessarily…because somebody's asking us but because it's important to our brand and the organisation we are' (Retail, UK).

Specific CSR initiatives are also described as drivers of reporting. For example banks, particularly in Australia, pinpointed the requirements of the Global Reporting

Initiative (GRI) Financial Services Supplement, coupled with competitor pressure, as a driver of their reporting on equal pay. Another described this influence as combining with internal factors.

The GRI coincided, I think, with heightened internal interest… because the figures had been tracked over some years and senior management was basically coming to the view that [progress] hadn't been as quick as it should've been. We'd had targets on female representation that went back a couple of years and they weren't being reached as quickly as we wanted…and there was also, from a CSR point of view, the need to have an appropriate framework, and GRI was selected. (Bank, Australia)

One interviewee described how their decision to report 'in accordance' with the GRI had led them to assess the GRI indictors. They found that most GRI indicators, including the diversity indicators, were useful measures of material interest to the company, and this was another reason for adopting these reporting frameworks.

Companies are trying to report that they are acting morally and responsibly: 'it's an opportunity for us to package a lot of what we do that we don't necessarily talk about, [but] we just do because it's considered the right thing to do as a large Australian employer'. Another explained that 'the message we're trying to give with [reporting on] gender diversity in general is: it's good business sense as well and you can have both'.

A significant influence of CSR reporting was noted in relation to bad news. As noted earlier, there had previously been little reporting of bad news on equal opportunities (Adams and Harte 1999). Our analysis of reports found that companies are now reporting some of this information, and this was explained by interviewees in terms of CSR: 'I suppose for lots of CR reporters, it's probably about accepting that it's reporting and reporting consistently [that matters], as opposed to only reporting if you've actually got progress or good enough detail'.

Interviewees with experience of sustainability reporting on other issues had learned that they could usefully report negative information if they followed it with an explanation of what they had been doing to address the issues raised, how their performance is improving and what they were planning to do next, confirming the findings of Grosser and Moon (2008). One interviewee commented:

the discussion with the CSR group is that, well, you're better to report it and be open about it now and then you can show in [the] next [report] how you're actually [doing] – so you're benchmarking against yourself. So in that sense I think it's better just to…admit that there [are] areas for improvement…[and to] demonstrate that, year on year, we are improving. (Bank, Australia)

Some interviewees believed that reporting bad news actually enhances both their sustainability reports and their reputation, because it shows that they can acknowledge problems and are trustworthy.

---

27. DeSimone (2008) believes that a fall in EEO reporting in the US, as noted by Calvert (2008), may be because of a decline in shareholder pressure on this issue as calls increase for broader sustainability reporting, which is often not aligned with US EEO disclosure requirements. This reveals the importance of ensuring that equality and diversity issues, including regulatory requirements, are effectively incorporated within CSR and SRI initiatives

Doing real comprehensive and transparent reporting is actually putting the good and the bad [in] because there might be reasons why you're bad in one area...you might be focusing somewhere else, or you might be in the process of fixing something or the data might be incomplete....The whole attitude that [you] don't put anything bad in because people will only focus on that, I don't think [that] is helpful, and... we don't necessarily have a problem putting bad information in...We often find [that] with trust in companies at an all-time low, the more bad information we put in the report the more people believe the good stuff. [If] you have a report that's all... brilliant performance across everything, people just [say] 'it's not true'. So if you're actually pretty honest about the areas [where] you're not doing well, people will accept that, well, maybe you are actually doing as well as the figures seem to indicate [somewhere else]. (Bank, Australia)

One interviewee contrasted the situation in the US where a company might well be sued for reporting certain bad news, with the more forgiving environment in Australia.

Finally, despite identifying significant drivers of reporting on gender equality, none of our interviewees described receiving significant feedback from stakeholder organisations on this issue, other than new recruits and shareholders at AGMs. One said: 'if you compare it to other issues that we might get asked about, it's...not significant' (Retail, UK). Nonetheless, once a company has a reputation on this issue, stakeholder interest can increase: 'any function that I ever go to, people always refer back to either the annual report or the stakeholder report and the focus that wo put on [diversity] and why we put the focus on that' (Banking sector). Feedback is important because it helps to determine the content of future reports. For a discussion of how these processes work see Chapter 6.

It appears to be the combination of different stakeholder interests that is driving more detailed reporting. Some explained their increasingly extensive reporting on diversity issues beyond HR, for example, as a way to communicate that they have gone beyond the basic talent management issues and are leveraging the benefits of a diverse workforce to create innovative outcome for the business.

We actually want to go beyond the visible aspects of diversity and say: can our senior women for, example, give a different perspective on growing the business. And so a lot of what we've done is...[to use] the innovation and creativity angle to say well, let's not think about targets, let's think how we make this mainstream as a business issue. (Bank, UK)

Reporting on equal pay provides an example of how interest from a range of stakeholders can combine to encourage reporting on sensitive issues. As well as being a legal requirement, accountability for equal pay is an issue in which civil society and government bodies have expressed a particular interest, and where the GRI and reporting by competitors have encouraged disclosure.

[The equal pay review] was a major piece of work and I think quite the first of its kind for this organisation. [Reporting]

sends a message that we're serious about it.... And I think it's one of those consistent issues that the public...and other stakeholders are interested in, especially when you take into account...the findings of reports published by the government and other organisations. (Bank, UK)

4.10 SUMMARY

Chapter 3 showed that regulation to report to government in Australia has played an important role in encouraging action, monitoring and internal reporting on gender equality in the workplace in many companies there. These developments have facilitated external reporting. The regulation has also acted as a prompt, or catalyst, which has helped companies to wake up to the business case for equal opportunity for women, which also drives external reporting. In these ways, regulation to report to government in Australia has been an indirect impetus to external reporting on gender/diversity, especially in companies that were not already effectively engaged with this agenda prior to the 1999 reporting regulation.

Even so, in Chapter 4 we saw that companies also explain reporting in terms of a response to changing demographic contexts, a shortage of labour, and the need to be regarded as an employer of choice. Overall, the increasing significance of market drivers was stressed most by our interviewees, particularly in the UK. They refer to recent socialisation of market forces, including employees, investors and, to a lesser extent, customers, as a reason to report externally on gender/diversity.

These forces are understood as being part of CSR. Interviewees describe a growing focus on gender and diversity in CSR reporting, which reflects civil society and government, as well as market influences. As one interviewee put it: 'There's a lot of drivers, I mean the government, the unions, the employer organisations, we're really all kind of moving to the same place on this' (Retail, Australia).

Sustainability and CSR reporting guidelines such as the GRI are specifically identified as drivers of reporting on gender issues, and our findings suggest that these may become increasingly influential. For example, the latest version of the *GRI Sustainability Reporting Guidelines* (GRI 2006), includes a core indicator requiring reporting on equal pay, covering 'Ratio of basic salary of men to women by employee category'. While equal pay was included in the earlier *Financial Services Sector Supplement* (GRI 2002a), its inclusion in the general guidelines for all sectors may act as a new external driver of reporting on this issue. [28]

28. The GRI, in collaboration with the International Finance Corporation (IFC), is in the process of developing a Gender Sustainability Reporting Resource Guide that will complement the GRI's Sustainability Reporting Framework (IFC Press Release 'IFC Partners with Global Reporting Initiative to Improve Corporate Reporting on Gender Issues', 17 September 2008, Washington DC).

5. Barriers to external reporting

In the previous chapter we examined the reasons why companies report externally on gender and diversity issues. In this chapter we look at the various reasons why they may not report, and the factors that inhibit the development of more extensive reporting of data available internally.

Some UK companies have been shown to withhold detailed information available internally on gender equality because of concerns that it does not reflect well on the company (Adams and Harte 1999; Grosser and Moon 2008). Interviewees in the Grosser and Moon (2008) study also described experiencing little demand from the public for more information, and had identified significant risks in revealing more than necessary. That study also found that companies often believe it better to report on a small number of KPIs than to provide a lot of data which address no specific objective. Problems of comparability of data were also noted. Our present study offered the opportunity to explore such reporting barriers in more detail.

5.1 DATA MONITORING AND RELIABILITY

Despite years of work on gender and diversity, many interviewees told us that their data collection and auditing systems continue to be a barrier to internal and external reporting. One interviewee from the oil and gas sector told us that because of numerous mergers it was difficult to collect comparable data and coordinate different data systems. Such difficulties had made it hard to establish basic information such as the percentage of women in the company's total workforce. Another explained that, while monitoring systems are quite advanced in the UK, availability of data from other parts of the business is more limited (see 5.2 below). One said: 'you always have to think, well is it worth asking [for] the data and having thousands of people walking round to get it? And that's why we've been focusing on the top leaders [only, in our reporting]' (Oil and Gas, UK)

In many companies, many of the data are still collected manually, which creates its own problems.

> How reliable is that data?...Like parental leave, [and] maternity leave retention rates, we have to manually do that, and so it's right for the EOWA [government monitoring] but I wouldn't take the next step and put it in an auditable CSR report...we're working on our data system to try and make sure we can get some of that fixed. (Bank, Australia)

Another said: 'there are things [about which] you can say..."Well that's roughly the number" but [it's not] verified...so we just have to exclude it' (Oil and Gas, UK). Some companies have solved this problem by putting un-audited data on company websites, or in specific hard-copy diversity reports, rather than in the audited hard-copy sustainability reports.

Others explained that data collection varies because business units are structured differently.

> We have a Head Office, [hundreds of] stores, [many] depots and the HR systems for those three key business areas,...supply chain,...stores and...Head Office. They're all quite different...Because the work patterns and the set-up of those organisations are very, very different. I mean the hours, for example, that people work are very different. So whilst I could quite easily get myself a figure for stores or get myself different figures for depots and supply chain, getting myself a figure which crosses the whole of the estate would be more of a challenge. (Retail, UK)

5.2 THE DATA ARE NOT COMPARABLE BETWEEN COMPANIES

Once data systems are well developed, perhaps the most important barrier to increased external reporting appears to be the incomparability of data between companies, even in the same sector. This lack of comparability, was described as a 'massive' barrier to further reporting (Retail, UK). Categories of staff are not always defined clearly and companies collect data in very different ways.

> Every company has different internal data management systems around human resources, so classifications are not necessarily consistent between companies...what we class as management and what the other banks class as management might be completely different, yet we get compared in terms of how we look. (Bank, Australia)

Others in this sector expressed similar reservations.

> We're very similar on what we report but very different on the actual metrics that we put around each indicator...so it's not easy to...make a comparison... [that we/or they] have more women in senior management...[Some] companies put their women on the board in with their executives...somebody else had actually merged executives and senior managers together. (Bank, Australia)

This presents a problem internally as well as externally, because:

> When we talk at diversity council level or at a management group level...someone looks at reports [from other banks] and says 'How come they can do that but we can't?' and then we've got to explain [that] we're measuring different things here. (Bank, Australia)

The retail sector is experiencing similar problems.

> There seems to be no parallel measures across our sector... for example, if you look at turnover...[this company includes] turnover of [all] people...but [another company] only report turnover of colleagues after one year's completed service...Now, obviously, turnover under one year is massive, because you've got students and all sorts of things like that...[so a] concern for reporting externally is that somebody can make their data look an awful lot better than yours....And people observe...[and] the media...[make comparisons]. (Retail, UK)

This interviewee continued:

> *I think there's an awful lot of anxiety around the fact that as there is so little parity in the way people measure some of these things, [so] why would we go external with [it]...what I would want, is for us to have an honest measure...that we would be able to stand up and defend and not have to...put lots of small print underneath...I am 100% confident that we are measuring in the same way but we're not reporting in the same way...And I don't know...how we can come to a position where everyone would say 'Right, okay, there is an accepted [way to report]...this kind of data, [and]...it's this'.* (Retail, UK)

One interviewee believed that her company was 'waiting to see more best practice amongst companies...what other companies are releasing [in our sector especially]' (Retail, UK).

One Australian interviewee explained that the problem of non-comparable data arises with government monitoring as well: 'I have this discussion every year with the EOWA [about]...what the definitions are around management, and...it's up in the air [still]'. She said 'I think you make it work for your own company in terms of...what initiatives you put in place to show a demonstrated change... within the culture of the organisation. But when you're being assessed by external parties, and...compared, then I think there's something missing' (Bank, Australia).

The same problems were noted in relation to measuring employee commitment and engagement: 'people use different scales and different theories in terms of how they measure employee engagement or commitment so you can't really compare apples with apples' (Bank, Australia). These problems apply to social reporting generally. A recent editorial in the business press noted that 'People are still waiting for social reports to look more like financial reports: more comparable figures, more order, and more generally agreed principles. These remain urgent priorities.' (*Ethical Performance* 2006: 12).

5.3 NEED TO REDUCE THE SIZE OF SUSTAINABILITY REPORTS

Many interviewees explained that the amount of information they could put in their sustainability reports was limited by space constraints: 'Our focus is about providing key facts of interest, not lots of detail' (Retail, UK). Another view was that:

> *We don't put everything in because...the report is already considered 60 pages too long, so we have increasing issues around materiality...and how to manage being appropriately transparent on all aspects of our performance without putting out a 120-page report. People are only going to read the one section that's relevant to them... Increasingly our thinking is that that would involve shifting away from just having the one big public annual report-type format and moving more to pushing a lot of this information online or into alternative communication channels.* (Bank, Australia)

5.4 BALANCING THE NEEDS OF DIFFERENT STAKEHOLDERS

It can be difficult to meet the information needs of different stakeholder audiences simultaneously: 'I think there's a pressure to find the appropriate balance that's most relevant to your key audiences and companies deal with this in different ways' (Bank, Australia). For example, companies may report different levels of data in their different reports and websites, or they may limit their reporting to details that are of interest to their main audiences only. One interviewee asked 'should we release the percentages [of different groups in the workforce] or should we just say whether we're green or red or amber?' (Retail, UK).

Another explained:

> *we've only got a certain amount of space for the people section which...has to meet our requirements in terms of external reporting and comparison and benchmarks to other organisations...we send [the reports] to regulators, NGOs, we get a lot of the rating agencies looking at them and in that sense it's a useful resource...[but] it's a difficult thing when you've got such a range of audiences.* (Bank, Australia)

Another interviewee from the banking sector agreed.

> *The challenge of a report like this is that your audience is quite broad so it's anyone from our customers to different government bodies, including ministers. We mail [our CSR report] to... ministers, associations, regulators, finance analysts, corporate responsibility analysts that do the ratings...potential employees [which we reach] especially via the website is another one...a big one... [and]...it's had a fantastic impact on staff.* (Bank, Australia)

Others said that concern for how internal stakeholders will react to information can constrain external reporting. One retail sector interviewee explained that they do not report targets for women in the workforce because these are disliked by some staff, and 'We don't want the managers to then go and discriminate against anyone' in an attempt to reach published targets. Rather, 'what we want to do is make people aware of where our opportunities are and as a business all work together to help move that forward' (Retail, UK). Also, external reporting by business units can, if the figures are not good, be discouraging to the people in these units where progress on gender equality is slow, particularly if representation of women in management, for example, is well below the UK average.

5.5 SUSTAINABILITY REPORTS HAVE A GLOBAL FOCUS

Several interviewees explained that although they wanted to increase the detail in their sustainability reports, these reports are designed to have a global focus: 'I've got to balance this as a global report' (Bank, UK). For example, when available data on gender is not as detailed overseas as it is in the UK, the more detailed UK information is often omitted, in order to ensure a balanced global report. This interviewee went on to say that, as they gather more information globally, they could conceivably report more detail for all countries. Nonetheless, they did not necessarily see the global sustainability report as the right place for this information. Another explained that more external reporting on gender issues is undertaken in countries where it is regulated (eg the US, Brazil, South Africa), but that such data are often not available for all operations.

5.6 WANTING TO REFLECT THE ORGANISATION IN A POSITIVE LIGHT

Fear of competitors constrains reporting: 'we've been happy to report on the stats as long as we're not including anything that would give a competitive advantage to others' (Retail, Australia). Companies are therefore reluctant to reveal more than their competitors.

> At the top level, they'd say 'Hang on, what's everyone else saying? Is this a good idea?...Is being transparent about this stuff going to...bring some kind of unwanted attention? (Retail, UK)

Fear of being seen in a bad light by other stakeholders has a similar constraining effect.

> Obviously from our CR point of view, we [can] always say 'you know, it's best practice [to report this]'. But obviously...if you get unwanted attention for something that isn't great news, commercially that's not a great thing. (Retail, UK)

This explains why releasing information about business units separately can be problematic, because a low level of women in management in one section can reflect badly on the whole company. (See also Chapter 4, page 42, on the role of CSR reporting with respect to the disclosure of negative information.)

5.7 EXTERNAL REPORTING CAN BRING INCREASED PRESSURE FOR ACTION

Staying silent on an issue is one way to avoid pressure to change. One interviewee said that reporting:

> puts the onus on us to actually do something about [the issue we are reporting on, especially] where the trend isn't as you would desire or where it's just plain bad... and I think that's a natural response. It hasn't stopped us from complying with GRI...but it's a question that I think the senior executives in particular asked quite reasonably, [saying] 'Well alright, this is what it says, what are we doing about it?' You can't just throw [information] out there in the public domain and not have some kind of idea of how you're going to respond. (Bank, Australia)

5.8 LITTLE DEMAND FOR FURTHER INFORMATION

As noted earlier, our interviewees do not appear to experience particular pressure from stakeholder groups to put more detailed information about gender in their sustainability reports (see also Grosser and Moon 2008): 'I really haven't had pressure from...any direction' (UK). Several other interviewees told us that they do not get requests for more information from stakeholders about gender issues. As one put it: 'at this stage...I sense a comfort level with the depth of data that we're making publicly available' (Bank, UK). This person felt that they could do more nationally based CSR reporting on these issues if they felt that there was a demand for it. Another explained:

> I can't produce these reports if they're going to be meaningless to people, it's a waste of people's time, so I have to find that...it's actually going to impact on either better employee commitment, better productivity, a push for better flexibility, there has to be a reason [or an external pressure]. (Bank, Australia)

Another said:

> We're finding there really isn't an audience for this enormous amount of information...it means not very much to anyone, apart from some people internally. (Retail, UK)

Lack of clarity about what further information would be useful to stakeholders discourages more detailed reporting: 'We have a general feeling that it would be good to report on more indicators but we haven't had anyone actually suggest what they might be' (Bank, Australia).

5.9 OTHER ORGANISATIONS ARE PROVIDING THE INFORMATION

Where there is a demand for information, other organisations may be providing it. One interviewee explained:

> I think at this stage there's enough [information],...those who really want to know the details...they can get that transparency through...the Auroras of this world, or through...the Top 50 Best Places to Work and that kind of thing...So I think the information is there. (Bank, UK)

(The organisations referred to here are market-based organisations or benchmarks.)

5.10 ORGANISATIONAL CULTURE

Lack of reporting was also explained with reference to organisational culture.

> Our general philosophy on life is that we don't go shouting about ourselves, we allow...the results to talk for themselves because...at the end of the day, if we serve our customers and they're happy and our staff are happy, we'll get on with life. (Retail, UK)

5.11 SUMMARY

Barriers to further reporting were described by interviewees in both the UK and Australia. These barriers included monitoring systems and data reliability, problems with comparability of data between companies, and limitations on the amount of detail that can be reported. There is a concern with presenting the company in a positive light. Indeed, this seemed to underscore concerns about the lack of comparability of data between companies. While some interviewees expressed a willingness to report more information despite fears about negative image, a lack of strong motivators for more detailed reporting was noteworthy, as was a lack of leadership to address the problem of comparability (see section 7.2, page 55). One interviewee described weighing up the demands for more data and the risks associated with reporting more, and finding little incentive to put further time and resources into collating and auditing more information for an external audience.

6. Processes of reporting

Companies collect a vast amount of data on gender and diversity. How they collect this data, and report it internally, in large part determines what they report externally. This chapter explores with our interviewees the processes that underpin reporting. In this chapter we:

- examine monitoring and internal reporting systems

- explore the processes used to determine external reporting content, which, we find, reflect the drivers identified in Chapter 3 (see page 33)

- include examples of innovative reporting on stakeholder engagement relating to gender/diversity issues.

When considering what to publish in external reports, one of the first considerations is the availability of information and data. Interviewees explained that they need information that is both comprehensive and auditable. Ideally this will have been measured consistently over a number of years to enable the identification of trends on the key issues. Thus, monitoring capacity informs the quality of external reporting.

Many of our interviewees indicated that their monitoring systems have developed significantly over the past five years, suggesting an increased management focus on gender equality. This has been essential to improvements in external reporting practice over the same period.

6.1 MONITORING SYSTEMS AND INFORMATION GATHERING

Even companies with the most advanced monitoring and internal reporting are continually improving their data collection systems, usually in order to improve internal management (see also Opportunity Now (2005) on this point).

Internal reporting of gender and diversity information generally takes place quarterly but can be monthly or six monthly. Sometimes this is in the form of business self-assessment systems that both collect data and initiate action. Some interviewees described board-level initiation of monitoring surveys. Data are generally reported to business unit heads, to senior management and to the board, albeit in varying amounts of detail.

Units of analysis

The unit of analysis for data collection and reporting is crucial. Detailed data at a particular business level are valuable because they enable action to be targeted where it is needed. The question is whether business unit, function, country or region is the most appropriate level of analysis. Many companies are still reviewing these choices. Even if a company chooses to monitor and report at the business unit level, problems remain, as different business units may have very different functions and roles. Thus, gendered data for different categories of workers may not be easily comparable with those in other parts of the

company. Several interviewees described attempts to align such disparate data systems within the company.

In the future the aim is [to] be able to provide each store with a [gender] breakdown of their store population. (Retail, UK)

This has implications for global reporting.

Because we now operate in a number of different countries, they want to have one system that every single country uses...We will not only be able to compare our data... in the UK, we'll also have the data available in every country we operate in. And we can all use and share that information and data in best practice. (Retail, UK)

The collection of global data on gender for internal reporting is a challenge.

That's something that has taken quite a lot of work to do. It's something that's... been requested by our board of directors...they want a gender breakdown and also main ethnicity categories as well. So for the first time, we're... reporting that for those countries with more than 1,500 employees, and that would be on a half-yearly basis. So it's going right to the top. (Bank, UK)

This company increasingly focuses on global lines of business, rather than geographical location, however, so it needs data by function or customer group. Some companies also monitor the extent to which their workforce mirrors the local community in terms of diversity and gender. One interviewee suggested that reporting should provide a national, local and regional focus as well as an international one.

Level of workforce monitored

Monitoring women's representation at management levels enables comparisons with the national averages. Interviewees described a growing interest within companies in the data on women in management, but the levels monitored vary considerably. One explained that the company had begun by monitoring women's representation at the group-leader level only, but has now extended monitoring to lower levels of management. It is increasingly common for companies to monitor the percentage of women at each work level, and compare this with national data.

Employee lifecycles and work–life balance

Many interviewees indicated that they collect gender-disaggregated data on recruitment, retention, promotion, training, and redundancy (ie throughout the employee lifecycle), but that this information is often not available throughout the business. Recruitment and turnover are often monitored by gender, both for full-time and part-time workers. One interviewee from the retail sector indicated that monitoring of promotions into different roles was conducted quarterly, by gender and age. Another said that:

we've had a good look at women's development and...we analyse our 360 data....We analyse how many women are going through our high-potential...leadership and development programmes, globally. (UK)

On the monitoring of flexible working one interviewee said:

we're just in a process of having a suite of diversity metrics which goes across not just gender but part-time, job share, telecommuting, all of those things that we have policies for, to start measuring them and to get some trends...by business unit. It'll be [reported] quarterly, so each business unit can then see where they're at, particularly with gender...so then they can see 'Oh, OK yes we do have a problem', rather than just saying 'Oh yes, we'll be OK'. (Bank, Australia)

This company is currently developing business-wide KPIs on these issues, but this can be challenging.

Our HR system has not been very good at picking up the flexibility issue so all [the information] we have is [about] part timers at the moment, in terms of numbers...But the mobility issue, and telecommuting and job-share numbers we've not been able to track. We do pick up that group of people in our staff perspective survey, which we do annually, and we assess how those people are feeling in relation to all the indicators, but we can't identify those people...But...coming next month, the month after, we will start tracking that. (Bank, Australia)

Targets

Data are often collected in relation to targets, whether or not these are externally reported.

Not only [have we] been monitoring how many [women] there are, but there have been targets set...aspirational targets...encouraging the regions [to] have more women. [These are negotiated] between each of the regions and their managers...And then they try to meet the targets... You've got targets by business and you've got targets by region. (Oil and Gas, UK)

These targets are monitored, with progress reported quarterly. Another UK interviewee explained the importance of targets for performance appraisal.

The UK probably leads the group...[and] this year for example, we have specific...targets for all our major departments in the UK, to reach a certain...percentage mix of promotions into senior management by the end of this year...by gender...and that's quite a bold move...[in] what people externally would probably perceive as quite a conservative organisation, so it is...right at the top of the agenda here... and those targets have been hardwired into performance appraisals, which ultimately determine the reward for those managers, [and] also their promotion. (Bank, UK)

Employee opinion surveys

Interviewees explained that they often need additional ways to assess progress beyond monitoring workplace profiles through data generated by their HR departments. Employee opinion surveys are commonly used for feedback and performance measurement. One interviewee explained that because their HR data system is outdated, they included questions in their employee opinion survey about age, ethnicity, gender, job categories and working hours to help ascertain their workplace profile.

Employee surveys can generate a fuller picture of progress, revealing, for example:

whether people are in fact even using all our policies. I mean we have fantastic policies but...are people able to use them? (Bank, Australia)

Not all employee surveys include questions about equality and diversity, but views are often solicited on related issues, such as various aspects of organisational culture. For example:

We ask a question about whether colleagues feel they are treated with fairness and respect, as this is one of our company values. (Retail, UK)

Responses are often monitored by gender. Another asks how staff rate their opportunity to progress within the company, and analyses women's responses separately. Business units may be required to address the issues raised in employee opinion surveys, including those on gender and diversity, and to report on progress to management.

Many companies conduct diversity and work–life balance surveys to assess satisfaction and morale among different groups. One interviewee (banking sector) explained that these are used to ascertain the number of staff with small children, for example, and their related workplace attitudes/issues. Another commented on a global company survey.

What was really interesting looking at the figures was in India childcare was relatively minor but elder care was huge. Sixty per cent of people said they were looking after an aged relative, and that was very useful information for us to have in terms of policies and so on. (Bank, Australia)

One interviewee reported a survey specifically on gender equality issues: 'We went out to the six main countries and said "Tell us what are the perceived and actual barriers for you?"' (Bank, UK). This research was invaluable in developing the company's gender equality programme. Companies also survey specific levels of the workforce (eg managers) on diversity.

One company admitted not being ready to do a full employee opinion survey:

it would be very useful to have this data regularly. But then the flip side of that is that if you're doing a survey [you can create] *some big expectation*[s] *and we've got to balance our ability to really deliver...action* [on] *everything that comes out of that survey. Probably at some point in the next few years we'll get to the point where we're happy doing that.* (Retail, Australia)

In the meantime the company uses data from focus groups to help monitor their progress.

Performance reviews and focus groups

Companies also use performance appraisal systems to learn about gender issues.

We took the data from the 360s [performance reviews], *we took about five years of data...and analysed* [them] *to look at what were the development issues that were different between men and women in the company...How might ratings differ between men and women* [and] *what the learning might be.* (UK)

Others use regular company-wide employee career discussions or exit interviews to capture data on gender. Focus groups for women also provide information about progress on gender equality.

There are a series of focus groups and listen-in sessions [on gender issues] *with...either...the CEO* [or] *the chief operating officer...And* [the results] *will be made internally available on the employee intranet...it's part of a more open sort of transparent environment...and quite a positive thing really* (Bank, UK)

Focus groups are regarded by some as providing better data than employee surveys 'because it's face to face and people can really explain... a view rather than just saying OK, a four out of five satisfaction [rate]' (Retail, Australia). This company holds focus groups in all divisions in order to evaluate the effectiveness of its policies. Employee networks for women or parents are also used to gain feedback on equality and diversity: 'The working parents group has certainly been quite active in providing information' (Bank, Australia). Others use mutual mentoring to 'give feedback directly from the younger women [to] the senior leaders' (Oil and Gas, UK).

6.2 INTERNAL REPORTING SYSTEMS

Once data on gender equality and diversity have been collected, to whom is it made available? Some companies make information derived from internal reporting widely available internally.

Referring to the Opportunity Now benchmark, a UK interviewee said:

we...put all...the detail for that submission on our global diversity intranet...so that all entities can learn the best practice...and learn from our successes and mistakes. (Bank, UK)

One Australian interviewee thought that they do not do enough with their EOWA report and that it would be good to publicise this more widely internally. Another described discussing the gender and diversity data regularly with their main union. On the other hand, one interviewee explained that communicating benchmarking data to their staff is not always effective as people cannot relate to percentages. Instead they communicate specific examples of women who have progressed in the company, to inspire others to follow suit.

Some interviewees indicated that scorecards and internal reporting sometimes generates competition between business units on gender and diversity, which was viewed as healthy and useful in driving progress: 'I've often found that the internal competition...has a lot [of] sway [when it comes to encouraging change]' (Australia).

Information is also provided to senior management: 'my boss would report on talent management to the board of directors and he would report on women:...our senior management groups one, two and three, globally, [showing]... the percentage of women in them [and in] the high-potential [talent] pool' (UK). At one company the data are sent:

out to all senior managers and their executive teams so that they see the full picture and not just for their function or brand...The material also goes to Board members so there is full visibility internally of that information. (Retail, Australia)

Managers are not only expected to report data to the Board, but sometimes also the actions they are taking in response. Others explained a similar dissemination of data widely across the company.

We have a [national] *work team, which is made up of representatives* [from] *right across the business, so from communications, from resourcing, from the customer team, and they all meet once a quarter...*[and] *they all get the data because that then drives their work plans for the coming year. And it also goes to...senior managers* [to inform] *their work plans...There* [are] *business updates as well that take place throughout the year, where this information's shared at resourcing sessions and talent plan meetings. So the information is used quite widely within the business.* (Retail, UK)

Another said:

I do a whole-of-enterprise quarterly women in management report which gets given up to the enterprise leadership team, to our top [managers] and group executives, and that happens on a quarterly basis and [this report]...has [an analysis of] a number of management roles split up by gender across all the businesses – what's changed from previous quarter to this quarter, how many numbers have changed, dropped, increased, where's been the impact, what's the return to work rates, what's the split across junior, middle, senior levels, specialist levels. So it's quite a detailed report that they get to review, how they're tracking in comparison to other parts of the business...This is something we've been doing for the last...five [or] six years...and it's something everyone continues to wait for, [they ask] 'When's it coming out again?' So it's something that they're used to getting now, and [which] they do value getting and looking at. (Bank, Australia)

One interviewee valued the internal reporting for its detail.

Particularly when you're looking at flexible workplace arrangements, a lot of women tend to come back to work in a part-time or contractual arrangement which is designated as specialist, so that might not be factored into the mainstream women in management reporting; so you might actually have more [women] than you think, women in reasonably senior roles; or you might have more women than you think [who are] not getting the same terms and conditions as a full-time employee because they're trying to make their work arrangements more flexible...the detail is where you get the most value from...reporting I think. (Bank, Australia)

6.3 EXTERNAL REPORTING

In this section we explore the processes that determine the content of external reports.

Internal reporting content informs the KPIs included in the external sustainability report. Increased global monitoring can expand external reporting but it can also involve extra work because, as one interviewee put it, there's 'a...grey area between internal usefulness and...making [the data] useful to an external audience' (Retail, UK). However, another said: 'We do quarterly reporting internally and there's no reason why we can't use that data on our website. So at the moment [most] data on our web is annual but we are looking to move that to quarterly' (Bank, Australia).

As noted in Chapter 3, companies may also use categories used by major CSR benchmarks and by their competitors when deciding the content of gender/diversity reports, as well as trying to identify and meet their own stakeholder expectations.

Benchmark models
The influence of CSR gender benchmarking organisations should not be underestimated: 'the breadth and depth of submissions for Opportunity Now will inform what we do... and we'll look at the trend [in terms] of what [other] external benchmarks are [requiring]' (Bank, UK). Although our research suggests that only a fraction of the submissions to Opportunity Now are used in external reporting, nevertheless one interviewee said: 'If they [Opportunity Now] dramatically changed their benchmarking, it would influence how I reported externally...because I may not be able to compare apples to...oranges, I might have to change the comparison' (UK).

Many interviewees said that the Global Reporting Initiative indicators (see GRI 2002b; GRI 2006) influence the content of their CSR reports. The gender criteria of the GRI financial services sector supplement (GRI 2002a), the BITC, FTSE4Good and Dow Jones Sustainability indexes, and the Reputex benchmarking system were all specifically mentioned by interviewees.

One interviewee explained how using data categories already developed for internal reports and external benchmarks reduces the work required in producing reports and information for external organisations: 'we try and line up [the data] so we're not duplicating or repeating ourselves' (Bank, Australia).

Competitors' corporate social reporting
Many interviewees described looking in detail at what other companies are reporting when deciding what to report themselves. This involves looking at national competitors, at companies in other sectors and, for Australian companies in particular, what companies report elsewhere in the world. This provides information not only about KPIs but also 'a good sense of the depth to which we need to go' (Bank, UK).

Stakeholder engagement and feedback
Some companies prioritise stakeholder feedback in deciding the content of reports.

I think first and foremost, it's stakeholder feedback... whether that's from formal mechanisms, such as the AGM, or...through direct requests coming in from shareholders or investors, etc. (Bank, UK)

Diversity managers and CSR teams share information about feedback on their gender and diversity reporting. Best practice in CSR, in this case stakeholder engagement about report content, is sometimes applied to reporting on gender and diversity issues.

One Australian interviewee explained that stakeholder engagement fills an important gap left by international reporting frameworks and benchmarks. In putting together the CSR report this company begins by looking at reporting frameworks, but because these are all international in focus:

then we do additional stakeholder engagement with Australian players, to assist us in two things: one, determining what are the most material issues for our immediate environment and market, and secondly... [asking] are there any issues which are not captured by these international frameworks that we also need to report on. (Bank, Australia)

The examples given of nationally specific issues did not include gender and diversity. However, this interviewee explained how CSR stakeholder engagement is now being extended to consultation on gender and diversity issues.

The range of organisations in Australia is not huge that are specifically focused on diversity issues and they tend to be focused on streams in diversity like disability, indigenous, that sort of thing.... But we also go out and talk to them, I mean we ask them...about stuff that we're doing, and if we're doing specific projects or initiatives then we often work with the organisations to get their feedback or input into it. (Bank, Australia)

Another explained that:

the Diversity & Inclusion Team is accountable for identifying the right partners, so they work with Catalyst [a US employer-led research organisation] and...those kinds of groups to define their strategy and what it is that they are going to be doing and what it is they are going to be reporting on. But they are not going to be talking to NGOs. (Oil and Gas, UK)

Leading companies have begun to include information about their engagement with stakeholders on gender/ diversity issues in their CSR reporting. Our analysis of reports and interviews suggests that direct engagement with women's organisations on reporting content is not common, but that best practice now involves incorporating them and other diversity organisations in reporting and auditing processes.

Interviewees also monitor press reports and government gender priorities, and one referred to being able to assure compliance with equal opportunities legislation.

Companies use feedback from staff surveys when deciding on the content of CSR reports: 'staff felt that women may not be equally represented at a management level but we hadn't really done a lot of communication around what the actual figures were' (Bank, Australia). Another explained: 'I guess the internal population, the[ir] reaction [to information published internally]...is actually the test of whether it would be good to put in the external [report]' (Oil and Gas, UK). Staff feedback on external CSR reporting is sometimes specifically sought. One company surveys the 200 or so people who contributed to the previous year's report. Another seeks union feedback.

Box 6.1 Examples of innovative reporting of stakeholder engagement on gender/diversity

Westpac report

• The Human Rights and Equal Opportunities Commission is included on its community consultation council, as well as representation from the Commonwealth Department of Family and Community Services.

Wal-Mart report

• 'Diversity Relations establishes and maintains productive, trust-based partnerships with women and minority stakeholder groups, community leaders and suppliers to continually improve Wal-Mart's reputation as a socially responsible enterprise' (Wal-Mart 2005: 14). It lists 15 women's organisations which Wal-Mart has met or supported.*

Tesco report

• Engaging with charities and NGOs in 2005/06, including Women on Farms in South Africa, and discussing flexible working with the Union of Shop, Distributive and Allied Workers (USDAW) (UK).

Ford report

• Its Sustainability Report Review Committee includes someone from Catalyst, a key US employer-led research organisation advising companies specifically on workplace gender equality issues. It reported that 'Ford's report should be applauded for addressing diversity and explaining how the issue is incorporated into its long-term business strategy' and advised that 'Future reporting can be improved by... strengthening the business case for diversity as part of its overall sustainability strategy.' (Ford 2005: 47)

* These are: American Women in Radio and Television; Business Women's Network; Catalyst; Center for Women's Business Research; Delta Sigma Theta; Gils, Inc; Hispanic Women's Corporation; International Women's Forum; League of Black Women; National Association of Women Business Owners; Network of Executive Women; Women Impacting Public Policy; Women's President Organization; Working Mother Media; National Council of Negro Women.

This year one of the key groups that we wanted to at least start with were the unions, and to actually say to them across the whole suite of people measures, from freedom of association through to diversity, 'what do you think of our reporting? Are we picking up on the key issues that you want to see us cover?', because they're one of our major stakeholders in terms of the people area. (Bank, Australia)

Companies disseminate CSR information to staff and to a variety of external stakeholders via the Web and the distribution of hard-copy reports. None specified dissemination to gender or diversity-related stakeholder groups.

Targets

Companies sometimes report against externally published workplace targets (see Chapter 2). One interviewee explained that while internal targets are set with business-level and country leader consultations, public targets on gender are global and this explains their global-level reporting practice. Australian interviewees explained how they often use their company EOWA reports to provide data for their external reports.

Who decides report content?

CSR departments play a major role in integrating and editing the gender and diversity content of company reports. Sometimes business units create their own CSR reports and then a CSR team or external relations department consolidates these into a single report. Similarly, the staff responsible for diversity often make suggestions about content.

My role in supporting the company's CSR process is to advise on what diversity metrics, programmes and activities we want to report on...We are part of a small team advising on what metrics and what initiatives we want to capture, as well as some case studies we want to showcase. (Retail, Australia)

One explained that: 'most of the stuff will get edited out anyway...[by] the communications people' (Australia). Senior staff may be involved in this process, including the head of HR and board members. Board CSR committees sometimes play an important role in editing and making final decisions about gender and diversity report content.

Report auditing

In a minority of cases the auditing of company reports specifically includes comments on gender and diversity information. For example, the Citigroup shareholder dialogue group gives feedback on its corporate citizenship reports. In 2005 Citigroup reported that 'While we have focused on the Environment section, we appreciate the inclusion of performance data on other factors, such as disclosure of Equal Employment Opportunity (EEO-1) US workforce diversity' (Citigroup 2005a: 6).

Mainstream auditors may comment on diversity issues. BP's Sustainability Report (BP 2005b: 33) includes an observation from its auditors, Ernst and Young, that 'Over half the sites visited this year had developed plans for diversity and inclusion in response to the findings of their Progress and Assessment Framework surveys and expressed a commitment to using diverse selection panels in recruitment decisions'. Ernst and Young also verify the company's data on group leadership diversity.

6.4 SUMMARY

Monitoring gender and diversity in the workplace involves a number of mechanisms beyond simply recording workplace profile data. Women's progression through the employee life-cycle may be recorded, and employee opinion surveys, performance appraisal data, exit interview data, focus groups, employee network feedback and research are also used to assess gender equality in the workplace. Data are generally reported regularly at a number of different business levels, including at the very highest. Many interviewees described a growing interest within the company in the data on women employees, and one described a growing interest in how many women are customers of the company. CSR departments often play a central role in deciding gender/diversity report content, as well as in auditing processes. For this reason one interview (Oil and Gas, UK) thought that the CSR and diversity departments needed to be more closely connected in her company.

Internal information is adapted for external reporting by all our interviewee companies. In addition, external CSR benchmarks now play a significant role in determining sustainability reporting on gender/diversity. We have found early signs of consultation with gender and diversity stakeholder groups on company reporting and auditing. Interest in these issues exists at board level in most of the sampled companies, and some board-level committees play a key role in deciding the content of external reports. CSR committees, at board level and below, are crucial in deciding report content, and CSR departments may solicit feedback about reporting on gender and diversity.

Finally, the evidence that the British Retail Consortium facilitates the sharing of best practice in equality and diversity monitoring among member companies suggests that these issues are now regarded as a mainstream concern.

7. The future of reporting

In this chapter we look briefly at our interviewees views on the future of reporting, and, in particular, what factors might drive reporting improvements.

7.1 REGULATION TO REPORT

We have seen some of the benefits derived from regulation to report to government in Australia, in terms of the impact upon company action and reporting (Chapters 3 and 4). One of the benefits of EOWA is that it gives guidance as to what issues to report upon to government, and how to report. We have noted that company reports to government are only partially available to the public, and that some interviewees argued that the EOWA should play an additional role in helping to advise upon and encourage best practice CSR reporting on gender issues.

Notwithstanding the evidence of CSR's powerful impact on gender reporting, we asked our UK interviewees for their views on government regulation or guidance on this issue. Several favoured government regulation on what to report. One believed that this would help the public become much better informed. Another said: 'I think it would be great!...I think it would be very interesting to have that kind of information. And I think it would radically change the way that some businesses operate.' (Retail, UK)

This interviewee thought it would be appropriate for companies to be mandated to report on equal pay in order to influence the worst offenders. Nonetheless, she believed that women in her company would not be greatly affected by such regulation because 'there's a lot of really genuine activity going on [already]'.

Others felt reporting regulation was not the best approach. One interviewee said that the fears associated with regulation to report on gender were mainly to do with the negative aspects of a compliance approach.

It's important for us to devise our own reporting mechanisms so that we can tailor them to our industry, our business and our needs. If government set reporting guidelines it could turn into producing stats for the sake of it rather than because we want to benchmark and improve our business. (Retail, UK)

Interviewees thought that business should be properly consulted before any government initiative.

I think as long as they went through a proper consultation process with the commercial industry and there was a collective view of how this might serve the interests of the government but also would be beneficial for those companies, then I couldn't see anything wrong with that. I think it would [help], I mean in terms of the greater transparency and best practice that we'd learn for starters...though, I guess the concern I would have would be...the creation of a new industry. (Bank, UK)

Another said:

I think nothing works as well as competition....I think that coming from the government again, yes, people would do it, you may end up with the lowest sort of bar but once things become a competitive issue and innovation and energy start being directed behind it, you see a lot more progress than you otherwise might. So I think...it [will] emerge as an area of competition...people are obviously very sensitive about what measures they're using and creating real parity between like companies. But if that were to...become a real...area of [competitive] focus, I think you would see [much more progress]. (Retail, UK)

This interviewee said it would take a proactive decision by her company, or another company in her sector, to take the lead and expose the rest, and drive competition. She felt that her company was in a good position to take such leadership because it has the funds to launch a big initiative, and has taken this role on other issues in the past.

We also found a number of people with very mixed views.

I just think that the more that we make people do things because they have to,...it doesn't work. And I think that's the problem with having monitoring. I suppose the other side of that is it does at least raise awareness, and if you're not doing something about a particular subject, for example women in management, then it forces you to do something. And sometimes you do need a kick and shove to do things. So I think there [are] two sides to the coin... it is a question of...how is the data verified, how is it checked, to make sure it is correct. But I do think it would encourage people to make sure that everyone was actively working on re-addressing the imbalance, I think that would be a good thing. (Retail, UK)

Another interviewee compared the UK regulatory environment on these issues with that in her home country, where: the government tracked company monitoring...and...government contracts very much depended on the monitoring. [This model] was very effective, let me tell you...you worked pretty hard at it'. Thus 'all companies were required to monitor, not just companies who wanted to be progressive'. (UK)

This interviewee described how such government action had long-term effects in terms of ingraining monitoring: 'My reaction when I initially came [to the UK] was "wow" – I'd never seen so much legislation with such little teeth'.

Our interviewees suggested that regulation can be most effective if it involves business and complements, or enhances, market drivers. One interviewee felt that Australian government regulation had tried to do just this by linking reporting to government to procurement contracts, and by providing practical benchmarking and reporting tools, developed with business input. Such tools have been created in the UK by business organisations such as Opportunity Now. In addition the Public Sector Duty to promote gender equality has begun to address equality criteria in government procurement processes, an issue which is being taken forward in the equalities bill published in June 2008.

7.2 REPORTING GUIDANCE AND THE ISSUE OF COMPARABLE DATA

Another option is for government to produce best practice guidance on this issue. One interviewee said: 'I think if there was...a template of what was [needed] in a public forum, I think it would make more companies accountable'. Asked if it would be useful to have more guidance about what civil society in particular wants, for example, this interviewee said: 'It is helpful because...then there's no argument about it'. Asked who might develop such guidance, the interviewee said: 'I would think the governmental equality organisations might be a good start'. (UK).

As noted in Chapter 5, one of the most prominent barriers to more detailed external reporting on gender equality appears to be the lack of comparability of data. In order to reduce this barrier, several of our interviewees recommended that reporting categories and KPIs, such as management grades, should be defined in much more detail by benchmarking organisations so that everyone is reporting on the same thing. One suggested that, rather than specifying categories that might be defined differently in different companies, reporting should be by salary group so:

instead of using the actual levels – executives or senior managers – you actually say what the pay rates are for that range, so you have $40,000–$70,000 [and]...$70,000– $150,000 [etc]. That might be perhaps a more transparent way of doing it. (Bank, Australia)

Others argued that reporting on exactly the same KPIs would not be easy, and one interviewee suggested that, instead, companies should more clearly define the categories which they choose to report on themselves.

If the descriptor is asking you as a company to specify exactly what you mean...that's easy to do and I think that's very good. [However] if you are asking us to report [any] particular kind of [data]... then that's a nightmare... because each company is thinking it through differently. And you can't ask them to all become the same because we've got different cultures, different industries and...that would be quite complicated. (Oil and Gas, UK)

Interviews addressed the question of whose role it should be to define such reporting categories. One interviewee believed that government needed to 'provide much more clarity and definition around what they're requesting companies to report [to government].' (Bank, Australia) Another believed that external CSR-type organisations should play the key role.

I think that that's really the role of external organisations like GRI to put more criteria around this so that we are measuring exactly the same things rather than quite different things, and it's only sort of one external outside body that can do that because it's not likely that we're [going to] get together with the other banks. (Bank, Australia)

Employer-led organisations were seen as a possible way forward. A UK interviewee regarded the British Retail Consortium (BRC) as potentially having an important role to play here. As retail sector companies compare their monitoring systems under the BRC umbrella she believed that they might also be able to come to some agreement about reporting, because:

it makes sense for everyone externally to be able to compare people and to look at the data and understand it...We do want to be able to release data externally. And we want to do it in a simple way that people understand and also that's in line with how other companies are reporting it. (Retail, UK)

Several interviewees believed that, at this stage, sector-specific reporting frameworks would be most feasible, and most useful for benchmarking.

Ultimately what we want is to be able to compare performance between companies within our sector... we'll start with getting base-line comparable, benchmarkable information, and then move to increasing levels of complexity if it's necessary, if it's relevant, and if we're asked to. (Bank, Australia)

In the longer term, cross-sector comparisons might be helpful, especially in attracting top-quality graduates into sectors such as retail.

Finally, agreed reporting categories can facilitate comparable reporting without limiting additional reporting. With regard to external reporting in the US, SIRAN (2005 Annex A: 2) notes that: 'some companies are concerned that EEOC job classifications do not represent their organisational structures. SIRAN encourages these companies to augment EEO-1 data with their own categorisations that are clearly explained. In this way, companies can present EEO information in a manner that they believe depicts their workforce composition accurately'.

7.3 OTHER KEY ISSUES

A number of other key barriers to reporting were identified by our interviewees. In particular, we note that limited space within CSR reports, and the need to address a variety of different stakeholders may lead to more Web-based reporting of these issues. This raises important questions about quality and verification of data. We found a lack of demand for more information, as perceived by companies, which raises questions about the participation of women's organisations and other equality bodies in stakeholder consultation and report auditing processes. These issues are addressed in our recommendations below.

Emulating good practice

Meanwhile our research revealed many examples of good practice that could be emulated (see also Chapter 2). Some of these are summmarised in Box 7.1.

Box 7.1 Examples of 'good practice' KPIs found in company reports

1. **Women's representation in the workforce, full-time and part-time employees, and hourly and salaried workers (numbers and percentages) covering:**

   - whole workforce

   - specific countries/regions

   - business units (sometimes including business units by country/region).

2. **Women in management: for the company as a whole, and for different business units and/or different countries.**

   - Numbers and percentages of women at each management category/level/salary level.*

3. **Percentage of women in the total workforce as compared with the percentage of women in management categories.**

4. **Recruitment**

   - Number/percentage of women recruits (different job categories).

5. **Career development**

   - Women as a percentage of full-time and part-time promotions between different levels of workforce and management.

6. **Work–life balance**

   Apart from reporting provision of flexible working options and childcare facilities best practice reporting includes quantitative performance data relating to parental leave, flexible working practices and childcare, such as:

   - employee satisfaction with work–life balance[29]

   - full-time/part-time transitions

   - maternity return rates for whole workforce/ business unit/country

   - numbers of families and children using its childcare centres/childcare allowance costs per annum by country.

7. **Diversity training**

   - Percentage of the management committee who have had diversity training.

   - Number of staff trained.

   - Awareness of diversity issues.

8. **Staff consultation**

   - Results from employee surveys on gender/ diversity. These sometimes include breakdowns by gender.

9. **Equal pay**

   - Comparison of average male and female salaries in senior management, management or pre-management categories by country.

   - Male-to-female ratios of fixed pay and total cash for different levels of the workforce.

   - Male and female salary differentials for different categories of workers and overall weighted average.

   - Whether male and female bonuses are comparable.

10. **Litigation**

    - Number of discrimination charges and expected costs.

11. **Gender in management appraisal**

    - Numbers of managers having diversity appraisals.

    - Whether performance in these is linked to compensation.

12. **Gender and other diversity identities**

    - Gender breakdown for different age categories by whole workforce/levels of management/country.

    - Gender breakdowns for different race categories for the whole US workforce at nine different levels (EEOC job categories).

13. **Board**

    - Number of women executives and non-executives on the board

14. **Awards and benchmark ratings on gender**

15. **Reports of auditing of gender/diversity data, and the inclusion of gender/diversity expertise in the process of stakeholder engagement about, or auditing of, company reports**

NOTES

It should be noted that the best reporting includes up to five years of consecutive data for some of these categories.

*Some US companies report according to the job categories that are required for EEOC reporting to government. These are: officials and managers, professionals, technicians, sales workers, office and clerical, craft workers, operatives, labourers, service workers.

---

29. Ideally this would be reported with a gender breakdown of data.

8. Discussion and recommendations

We have examined the extent and nature of reporting on women's employment issues in a sample of the largest companies in Australia, the UK and the US. Although the small sample size of our study means that our findings are not statistically representative of wider business practice, they are indicative of the practices of some of the largest companies in the world.

Our content analysis of company reports and websites elicited some detailed and extensive performance reporting on gender equality in the workplace in all three countries, as well as much reporting on programmes of action to address this issue. The findings signal considerable progress against UK data from a decade ago, confirming and extending the findings of Grosser and Moon (2008).

We found that reporting is broadly comparable across all three countries, although collectively Australian companies report less information on this issue than their UK and US counterparts. Improved disclosure in the UK is illustrated by the extent of reporting on the employment and advancement of women which now appears comparable to, rather than lagging behind, that in the US.

Most performance reporting refers to women's employment patterns/workplace profile. It is much more limited with respect to workplace issues such as recruitment, retention, career development and training. It is possible to track progress in this area in many companies by examining the reporting of performance data on the gender equality issues they have chosen to prioritise. A minority of companies now report information relating to issues that are a priority for civil society and government, such as equal pay, litigation and women's representation in non-traditional jobs. This is particularly true of equal pay, where CSR reporting systems (eg the GRI) have given an impetus to increased transparency. Nonetheless, the lack of comparable reporting systems and KPIs means that meaningful comparisons and benchmarking between companies based on publicly reported data are limited, even for issues on which nearly all companies report (eg women's representation in management), and even between companies in the same sector.

Our study has also involved interviews with managers, particularly about motivations for and processes of reporting. We found that external reporting depends on internal monitoring of gender equality, which appears to have developed significantly over the past five years in order to improve management of these issues. This further illustrates a growing business focus on gender equality.

What I want to make clear is we don't pretend to have got this right but in terms of where we've come from since the nineties...I think we have made some progress...at least now we have a recognition that this issue's on the table and we have some support from the very top of the organisation, which is great. (Bank, UK)

When we investigated the reasons companies don't report in more detail, we found that lack of frameworks for ensuring that data reported are comparable among companies is a major barrier to increased reporting. Interviewees also referred to concerns with their monitoring systems and reliability of data; space limitations of reports; the fear of presenting the company in a negative light; the lack of pressure to report more.

Turning to our interest in the respective impacts of regulatory and voluntary approaches to equal opportunities reporting we explored whether the obligation of US and Australian companies to report to governments leads to better public reporting.

The requirement for companies to report to government in Australia appears to have had an indirect impact on external reporting. We learnt that the regulation has driven monitoring and internal reporting on gender equality in all companies where this was not already a management focus. These developments have, in turn, facilitated internal progress on gender equality, and informed external reporting. The regulation has also acted as a prompt to make companies more aware of the business case for equal opportunity for women, which we found also motivates external reporting. The requirement to report to government has not significantly affected companies that were already focused on advancing women in the workplace.

Company transparency and accountability on gender equality is not mediated through company reports alone. The regulation in Australia does contribute to public accountability through the availability of company annual returns on the EOWA website. While some elements of these reports remain confidential, companies often provide much more information via this government forum than they do in their own reporting to the public. Companies that have performed well by EOWA criteria have their obligation to report waived for three years, however, which can be considered as a lost opportunity for government to promote current best practice.

The US regulation to report equal opportunity employment data to government is more long-standing. Although we did not interview US companies, we did find evidence from their reports that data reported to government are also used in public reporting, and that the availability of aggregate data reported to government enables companies to report against industry benchmarks. In addition, press releases reveal that the existence of monitoring returns on gender equality in the workplace has helped civil society organisations and shareholders to call for improved accountability on this issue (eg Wal-Mart, Home Base).[30]

---

30. The decline in public reporting of EEO performance data submitted to government in recent years (Calvert 2008) suggests that the requirement to report to government will not on its own lead to greater transparency to the public'

Overall, our research suggests that regulation to report to government is not a necessary or sufficient condition for external reporting, and that a more complex picture of motivation for reporting emerges.

Turning to our interest in whether and how the new wave of corporate social responsibility has informed corporate social disclosure on gender equality in the workplace, we found that gender and diversity have become central elements of CSR and of CSR reporting. Most reporting on gender issues takes place within CSR reports and websites.

Interviewees explain these trends with reference to changing demographic contexts and changing expectations of employees, potential recruits, investors and, to a lesser extent, customers. These findings are consistent with the 'socialisation of markets', which we have identified as crucial to the growth of CSR over the last 10 years.

Our interviewees indicated that CSR reporting and benchmarking systems (eg the GRI) have shaped reporting on gender issues. Companies even compete with each other to have the best CSR reporting, including on gender and diversity issues, and these issues are perceived as increasingly important for corporate reputation (another motivator of CSR).

Similarly, we found that company CSR departments and committees play vital roles, along with diversity and HR departments, in identifying stakeholder interests and editing and producing CSR reports. CSR stakeholder engagement is beginning to include gender and diversity issues. Some interviewees felt that these two departments needed to be more closely connected. The fact that CSR systems are less well developed in Australia than the other two countries helps to explain why the reporting of gender issues is less well-developed among Australian companies.[31]

Many interviewees referred to the simultaneous influence of a range of drivers.

> It's almost the coming together of lots of different influences and the business...swivels in that direction and [says] 'Right, okay, this is on the radar, what are we going to do about this?'. (Retail, UK)

This final comment seems to capture our findings about leading companies and the reporting of gender equality in a nutshell.

8.1 RECOMMENDATIONS

Both legislative and non-legislative mechanisms are important in the process of improving equal opportunities monitoring and reporting to the public. Previous studies have recommended mandatory public reporting, and it seems that this approach may well still be necessary. We found that regulation to report to government has played a critical role in driving action and reporting on gender issues in some companies, suggesting that regulation for broader public reporting, if ever enacted, could have a similar affect. Given the lack of such regulation in the countries we looked at, our study could not test the efficacy of such legislation, and our interviewees had mixed views on this issue.

Significantly, we also found that market, civil society and government drivers for greater CSR have been very influential with regard to company action and public reporting on gender issues. Not only did our interviewees tell us this, but we found that reporting has improved significantly in the UK (the country for which we had substantial prior data) in the absence of regulation.[32]

Public reporting in all three countries is unsystematic and idiosyncratic, which limits accountability. One of our main findings was that there is an urgent need for clear guidance on reporting categories and how to measure them, in order to enable meaningful comparisons to be made between companies. Notwithstanding the benefits that arise when more companies adopt gender indicators, problems of clarification and comparability mean that further disclosure innovation is needed. There is considerable scope for improving reporting, and therefore accountability, through the development and use of widely accepted key performance indicators. We have found significant interest in further guidance on, and agreement over, best practice reporting in this area in both the UK and Australia. In Australia this was considered necessary with regard to reporting to government, as well as reporting to the public.

We note that regulation to report to government can help in this regard, for where it requires reporting on specific categories of workers (as in the US, for example) these categories can be used in public reports, and for benchmarking purposes. CSR benchmarks, such as that run by Opportunity Now in the UK, provide similar guidance. Thus, help might be provided by government, business organisations such as Opportunity Now, or CSR organisations (eg GRI), trade unions and NGOs. Processes involving all these organisations are likely to be most effective. While the debate as to whether or not to regulate for public reporting on social and environmental issues continues, our study indicates several other important and complementary avenues for improving reporting practice.

---

31. As noted in footnote 2, research has shown that large companies are more likely to report on CSR issues. Our sample consisted of the largest companies in each country, however the Australian companies were, on average, considerably smaller than the UK and the US companies in our sample, which may also partly explain why the Australian companies collectively reported less information.

---

32. Research has shown that large companies are more likely to report, which may partly explain the fact that Australian companies in our sample reported less information, and also suggests that regulation to report to government, or to the public, may have a greater impact on small companies than large ones.

These are the focus of our recommendations, which are as follows.

1. Companies should routinely report gender-disaggregated HR data. While companies will always report on HR with different priorities, reporting their key HR performance indicators with gender breakdowns will have the effect of immediately increasing transparency on gender equality.

2. Our study has revealed a quite urgent need for standardised reporting KPIs. We recommend that a governmental organisation, a representative business association or an accounting body take the lead on identifying agreed best practice guidance for corporate public reporting on gender workplace issues.

   • This needs to provide both consistent and comparable key reporting indicators and agreed ways of measuring them.[33]

   • This would be best taken forward through a multi-stakeholder approach involving collaboration with the GRI and other CSR initiatives and organisations; businesses and trade associations such as the British Retail Consortium; unions, and employees more generally; civil society organisations, in particular leading women's NGOs; social accountants; government.

   In particular, indicators will need to reflect regulation and the work of the equal opportunities commissions, the EOWA, and the Government Equalities Office (UK), for example. This would help to ensure that corporations not only show legal compliance, but contribute to the realisation of wider governmental priorities for gender equality.

3. In Australia, the EOWA should consider helping to improve corporate accountability to the public by commenting on or evaluating company CSR reports on gender equality in the workplace.

4. Ways need to be found to increase the capacity of civil society organisations to inform companies better about their expectations on gender reporting and thereby to enhance their impact as stakeholders. Both government and business could take initiatives in this regard, for example, by offering training for gender-related NGOs on CSR and CSD issues.

5. Companies may need to anticipate some scepticism about those website reports, updates and news flashes on gender workplace issues that are not clearly verifiable or audited. We recommend that stakeholders are invited to review and give feedback on gender reporting, and that this feedback is included as part of the external audit of the sustainability report.

6. CSR and sustainability reporting awards should extend to gender equality/diversity reporting. These could be sponsored by government agencies (eg EOWA), business organisations (eg Opportunity Now), or accounting bodies and CSR organisations (eg ACCA).

---

33. The 23 items in Chapter 1 (see page 11) could provide a good starting point for discussion as these have been identified with reference to numerous stakeholder interests.

Appendix 1:
Examples of gender and diversity awards and benchmarks referenced in the sampled company reports

Alfred P. Sloan Award for Business Excellence in Workplace Flexibility (US)

Australian Chamber of Commerce and Industry and Business Council of Australia National Work and Family Awards (Australia)

National Institute of Women, Gender Equality Model (Mexico)

Business in the Community Awards for Excellence (UK)

European Federation of Black Women Business Owners (EFBWBO) Black Women in Business Awards (EU)

Business and Professional Women Employer of the Year (US)

Castle Awards (UK)

Catalyst Awards (for efforts to advance women leaders) (UK)

CNN.com, Top 10 Companies to Work for in America (US)

DiversityInc magazine's Top 50 Companies For Diversity (US)

EOWA awards (Australia)

- EOWA Employer of Choice for Women
- EOWA Business Achievement Award: Most Promising Organisation for the Advancement of Women
- EOWA Leading CEOs for the Advancement of Women
- EOWA Leading Australian Organisation for the Advancement of Women (>500 Employees)

Exame magazine's The 150 Best Companies to Work For

Executive Leadership Council Corporate Award for Leadership in Advancing Diversity in Corporate America (US)

Female FTSE Index (UK)

Forbes.com, The 100 Most Powerful Women (US)

Fortune Magazine's Top 50 Employers for Women (US)

GenderPAC 2005 National Corporate Achievement Award (US)

Great Place to Work Institute, Best Workplaces, including 30 Best Companies to Work For (UK, US), and Best Place to Work (EU)

Higginbotham Corporate Leadership Award (for long-standing commitment to corporate diversity) (US)

Management Today magazine's HR Excellence Award (UK)

Human Rights Campaign's Corporate Equality Index (US)

Inroads – Frank C. Carr Award (recognises an individual or corporation for their work on workforce diversity and in the community) (US)

League of Women Voters, Edith L. Stunkel Good Government Award (US)

National Association of Women Lawyers, President's Award (US)

Opportunity Now City Focus Award, and ratings in the Opportunity Now benchmark (UK)

The *Sunday Times* 100 Best Companies to Work For (UK)

Tommy's Parent Friendly Awards (UK)

US Banker Ranks, The 25 Most Powerful Women In Banking (US)

VISTA magazine's America's Top Family Friendly Companies (US)

Women of Achievement Award (Australia)

Woman Engineer #1 Company (US)

Working Mother magazine's Hall of Fame of 100 Best Companies/100 Best Companies for Working Mothers (US)

YWCA Academy of Women Leaders (US)

Since this research was carried out new benchmarks have been created, such as *The Times* 'Where Women Want to Work Top 50' (UK).

Appendix 2:
Examples of CSR awards and benchmarks referenced in the sampled company reports

AccountAbility Rating of the Global 100 Companies (UK)

Australian Human Resources Institute, Australian Human Resources Awards (Australia)

Australian SAM Sustainability Index (Australia)

Great Place To Work Institute, 50 Best Places to Work (Brazil)

Business in the Community CR Index (UK and Australia)

Dow Jones Sustainability Index (US)

Equator Principles (International)

European Commission *Managing Change* report (which requires reporting on equal opportunities) (EU)

FTSE4Good Indices (UK)

Global 100, 100 Most Sustainable Corporations in the World (Canada)

Global Sullivan Principles (International)

Great Place to Work (various national listings)

GRI *Guidelines* (International)

GRI's *Financial Sector Supplement: Social Performance* (International)

Investors in People (UK)

Johannesburg Stock Exchange Index (South Africa)

Reputex Social Responsibility Rating (Australia)

Storebrand Best in Class (Norway)

Sunday Times Best Companies to Work for (UK, Europe, US)

SustainAbility's Global Reporters' survey (UK)

UN Global Compact (International)

OTHER STANDARDS REFERRED TO

ILO (International Labour Organization) Declaration of Fundamental Principles and Rights at Work

OECD (Organisation for Economic Co-operation and Development) Guidelines for Multinational Enterprises

Six-sigma Management Quality Tool. Six-sigma is a well known quality management system or tool.

References

Adams, C. (2002), 'Internal Organisational Factors Influencing Corporate Social And Ethical Reporting: Beyond Current Theorizing', *Accounting, Auditing & Accountability Journal*, 15 (2): 223–50.

Adams, C., Coutts, A. and Harte, G. (1995), 'Corporate Equal Opportunities (Non-) Disclosure,' *British Accounting Review*, 27: 87–108.

Adams, C. and Harte, G. (1998), 'The Changing Portrayal of the Employment of Women in British Banks' and Retail Companies' Corporate Annual Reports', *Accounting, Organization and Society*, 23 (8): 781–812.

Adams, C. and Harte, G. (1999), *Towards Corporate Accountability For Equal Opportunities Performance*, Occasional Research Paper No. 26 (London: CAET).

Adams, C. and Harte, G. (2000), 'Making Discrimination Visible: The Potential for Social Accounting', *Accounting Forum*, 24 (1): 56–79.

Adams, C. and Frost, G. (2004), *The Development of Corporate Web-sites and Implications for Ethical, Social and Environmental Reporting through these Media*, Institute of Chartered Accountants of Scotland (ICAS) research monograph (Edinburgh).

Adams, C. and McPhail, K. (2004), 'Reporting and the Politics of Difference: (Non) Disclosure on Ethnic Minorities', *ABACUS*, 40 (3): 405–35.

Australian Government Department for Environment and Heritage (2005), 'The State of Sustainability Reporting in Australia 2005' [online text], <http://deh.gov.au/settlements industry/corporate/reporting/survey.html>, accessed February 11 2007.

Aspen Institute (2008), *Beyond Grey Pinstripes* [website], <http://www.beyondgreypinstripes.org>, accessed 22 September 2008.

Aurora (2008a), *Where women want to work* [website], <http://www.wherewomenwanttowork.com>, accessed 22 September 2008.

Aurora (2008b), The *Times* 'Where Women Want to Work Top 50' [online text], <http://www.wherewomenwanttowork.com/top50/top50/interest.asp>, accessed 22 September 2008.

Aviva (2006), *Corporate Social Responsibility Report 2005* [online report], <http://www.aviva.com/csr05>, accessed 10 October 2008.

Batten, J. and Birch, D. (2005), 'Defining Corporate Citizenship: Evidence from Australia', *Asia Pacific Business Review*, 11 (3): 293–308.

Best Companies (2008), *The Sunday Times 'Best Companies to Work For'* [online text], <http://www.bestcompanies.co.uk//list_intro.aspx>, accessed 22 September 2008.

BHP Billiton (2005a), *A Sustainable Perspective: BHP Billiton Sustainability Report 2005* [online text], <http://sustainability.bhpbilliton.com/2005/repository/aboutReport/aboutReport.asp>, accessed 10 October 2008.

BHP Billiton (2005b), 'HSEC Management Standards', *Management Systems Review* [online text] <http://sustainability.bhpbilliton.com/2005/repository/governanceSustainableDevelopment/ourPerformance/managementSystemsReview.asp>, accessed 10 October 2008.

Birch, D. (2002), 'Corporate Citizenship in Australia: Some Ups, Some Downs,' *Journal of Corporate Citizenship*, Issue 5 (Spring).

BITC (Business in the Community) (2005), *Corporate Responsibility Index Survey* (London).

BP (2005a) *Making Energy More: Annual Report and Accounts 2005* (London).

BP (2005b) *Making Energy More: Sustainability Report 2005* (London).

Cable News Network (2008), '100 Best Companies to Work For', *Fortune* [online magazine] (4 February 2008), <http://money.cnn.com/magazines/fortune/bestcompanies/2008/full_list/index.html>, accessed 23 September 2008.

Calvert (2004), 'The Calvert Women's Principles: A Global Code of Conduct for Corporations,' (Bethesda, MD: Calvert Group) [online text], <http://www.calvert.com/womensPrinciples.html>, accessed June 07.

Calvert (2008), *Examining the Cracks in the Ceiling: A Survey of Corporate Diversity Practices in the Calvert Social Index* [online report], <http://www.calvert.com/pdf/CorporateDiversity2008.pdf>, accessed 10 November 2008.

Catalyst (2008), *Catalyst Award* [online text], <http://www.catalyst.org/page/54/catalyst-award>, accessed 29 September 2008.

CCMAC (Commonwealth Corporations and Markets Advisory Committee) (2006), *Inquiry on the Social Responsibility of Corporations* (Canberra).

CIPD (Chartered Institute of Personnel and Development) (2005), *Human Capital Reporting: An Internal Perspective* [online PDF report], <http://www.cipd.co.uk/NR/rdonlyres/14186133-F440-47DF-92BE-36E5F65B7962/0/humancapguide0105.pdf>, 22 September 2008.

Citigroup (2005a), *Citizenship Report* (unspecified).

Citigroup (2005b), *Diversity Annual Report* (unspecified).

Cooper, C. and Puxty, A. (1996), 'On the Proliferation Of Accounting (His)tories', *Critical Perspectives on Accounting*, 7: 285–313.

DTI (Department of Trade and Industry) (2003), *Accounting for People Report* (London).

DTI (Department of Trade and Industry) (2004), *The CSR Competency Framework* [online PDF report], <http://www.bitc.org.uk/document.rm?id=5102>, accessed 23 September 2008.

Economist (2005), 'CSR and the Good Company,' 22 January 2005: 13.

EOC (1985), *Code of Practice for the Elimination of Discrimination on the Grounds of Sex and Marriage and the Promotion of Equal Opportunity in Employment* (London: Equal Opportunities Commission).

EOWA (Equal Opportunities for Women in the Workplace Agency) (2008), *EOWA EOCFW Criteria and Prerequisites – 2007 Onwards* [online PDF document], <http://www.eowa.gov.au/EOWA_Employer_of_Choice_for_Women/What_is_EOWA_Employer_of_Choice_for_Women/Information_Kit/Criteria_and_Prerequisites.pdf>, accessed 29 September 2008.

Equal Pay Act (1970), [online PDF],< http://www.opsi.gov.uk/acts/acts1970/PDF/ukpga_19700041_en.pdf>, accessed 22 September 2008.

Ernst and Ernst (1978), *Social Responsibility Disclosure* (Cleveland).

Ethical Performance (2006), December (Canterbury: Dunstans Publishing).

Finance Sector Union (Australia) (2005), (untitled), press release, Monday 7 February.

Forbes (2008), 'The Forbes Global 2000' [online text], <http://www.forbes.com/2005/03/30/05f2000land.html>, accessed 22 September 2008.

Ford (2005), *Our Route to Sustainability, Connecting with Society – Ford Sustainability Report 2004/5* [online PDF report], < http://www.ford.com/doc/2004-05_sustainability_report.pdf>, accessed 10 October 2008..

Freeman, R. E. (1984), *Strategic Management: A stakeholder approach* (Boston: Pitman).

Freeman, R. E., Harrison, J. S. and Wicks, A. C. (2007), *Managing for Stakeholders: Survival, Reputation, and Success* (Yale University Press).

General Electric (2005), 'Letter to Stakeholders', *Annual Report 2005* (unspecified).

General Electric (2006), *Citizenship Report* (unspecified).

General Motors (2005), 'GM Corporate Responsibility Report' [online text], <http://www.gm.com/company/gmability/sustainability/reports/05/700_social/3_thirty?>, accessed 23 June 06.

Government Equalities Office (2008), *Framework for a Fairer Future – The Equality Bill,* June 2008 (available at www.equalities.gov.uk) (London).

Gray, R. (2006), 'Social, Environmental And Sustainability Reporting And Organisational Value Creation. Whose value? Whose creation?', *Accounting, Auditing & Accountability Journal,* 19 (6): 793–819.

Gray, R., Owen, D. and Adams, C. A. (1996), *Accounting and Accountability: Changes and Challenges in Corporate Social and Environmental Reporting* (London: Prentice Hall).

Gray, R., Owen, D. and Maunders, K. (1987), *Corporate Social Reporting* (Hemel Hempstead: Prentice Hall).

Great Place to Work Institute UK (2008), *UK's 50 Best Workplaces* [online text], <http://www.greatplacetowork.co.uk/best/list-uk.htm>, accessed 22 September 2008.

GRI (Global Reporting Initiative) (2002a), *Financial Services Sector Supplement: Social Performance* [online report], <http://www.globalreporting.org/NR/rdonlyres/B1EF2733-3BC7-4916-819F-AF837AC6F8FB/0/SS_FinancialServicesSocial_ENG.pdf>, accessed 12 February 2007.

GRI (Global Reporting Initiative) (2002b), *Sustainability Reporting Guidelines* (Amsterdam).

GRI (Global Reporting Initiative) (2006), *Sustainability Reporting Guidelines*, Version 3 (Amsterdam).

GRI (Global Reporting Initiative) (2008), *Reporting Framework* [online text], <http://www.globalreporting.org/ReportingFramework/>, accessed 29 September 2008.

GRI (Global Reporting Initiative) (2008b), *Corporate reporting of gender issues come under the spotlight in combined IFC/GRI project,* press release (23 September 2008) [online text], <http://www.globalreporting.org/CurrentPriorities/GenderandReporting/GenderProjectNews.htm>, accessed 29 September 2008.

Grosser, K (forthcoming), 'CSR and Gender Equality: Women as Stakeholders and the EU Sustainability Strategy', *Business Ethics: A European Review.*

Grosser, K. and Moon, J. (2005), 'Gender Mainstreaming and Corporate Social Responsibility: Reporting Workplace Issues', *Journal of Business Ethics*, 62 (4): 327–40.

Grosser, K. and Moon, J. (2008), 'Developments in company reporting on workplace gender equality? A corporate social responsibility perspective', *Accounting Forum*, 32: 179–98 .

Henderson Global Investors (2002), *Socially Responsible Investment: Closing Britain's Gender Pay Gap* (London).

HBSC (2005), *Corporate Social Responsibility Report 2005.* <http://www.hsbc.com/hsbc/csr/csr-at-hsbc/faqs> accessed 4 May 2006.

Kalev, A., Dobbin, F. and Kelly, E. (2006), 'Best Practice or Best Guesses? Assessing the Efficacy of Corporate Affirmative Action and Diversity Policies', *American Sociological Review*, 71: 589–617.

Kingsmill, D. (2001), *A Review of Women's Employment and Pay* (London: Women and Equality Unit, Cabinet Office).

KPMG (2005), *International Survey of Corporate Responsibility Reporting* (Amsterdam).

Matten, D. and Moon, J. (2004), 'Corporate Social Responsibility Education in Europe,' *Journal of Business Ethics* 54: 323–37.

MacCarthy, J. and Moon, J. (forthcoming) 'CSR Consultancies in the United Kingdom' in Galia, C. ed. *Consulting for Sustainability* (London: Greenleaf).

Moon, J. (2002), 'Business Social Responsibility and New Governance,' *Government and Opposition* 37 (3): 385–408.

Moon, J. (2003), 'Socializing Business?' *Government and Opposition* 38 (2): 265–73.

Moon, J. and Muthuri, J. (2006), *An Evaluation of Corporate Community Investment in the UK* (London: Charities Aid Foundation).

Moon, J. and Sochacki, R. (1998), 'New Governance in Australian Schools: a Place for Business Social Responsibility?' *Australian Journal of Public Administration*, 55 (1): 55–67.

Moon, J. and Vogel, D. (2008), 'Corporate Social Responsibility and Government,' in: Crane, A., McWilliams, A., Matten, D., Moon, J. and Siegel, D. (eds) *The Oxford Handbook of Corporate Social Responsibility* (Oxford: Oxford University Press).

OECD (Organisation for Economic Co-operation and Development) (2000), *OECD Guidelines for Multinational Enterprises* [online PDF], <http://www.oecd.org/document/28/0,3343,en_2649_34889_2397532_1_1_1_1,00.html>, accessed 22 September 2008.

Opportunity Now (2001), *Equality and Excellence: the Business Case* (London).

Opportunity Now (2004), *Diversity Dimensions, Integration into Organisational Culture* (London).

Opportunity Now (2005), *Line Managers and Diversity: Making It Real, Opportunity Now*, (London: Business in the Community).

PJCCFS (Commonwealth Parliamentary Joint Committee on Corporations and Financial Services) (2006), *Corporate Responsibility: Managing Risk And Creating Value*, Commonwealth of Australia, June.

Porter, M. and Kramer, M. (2002), 'The Competitive Advantage of Corporate Philanthropy' *Harvard Business Review,* December.

Royal Bank of Scotland (2004), *Corporate Responsibility Report* (Edinburgh: RBS Group).

Royal Bank of Scotland (2005a), *Diversity and Inclusion report* (Edinburgh: RBS Group).

Royal Bank of Scotland (2005b), *Annual Report* (Edinburgh: RBS Group).

Sainsbury (2005), *J. Sainsbury plc Corporate Responsibility Report, 2005* (London).

Sex Discrimination Act (1975), [online PDF document], <http://www.opsi.gov.uk/acts/acts1975/PDF/ukpga_19750065_en.pdf>, accessed 24 September 2008.

Shell (2005a), *The Shell Sustainability Report 2005* [online PDF report], <http://www-static.shell.com/static/responsible_energy/downloads/sustainability_reports/shell_report_2005.pdf>, accessed 24 September 2008.

Shell (2005b), *Royal Dutch Shell plc 2005 Annual Report and Form 20-F* [online PDF report], <http://www-static.shell.com/static/investor/downloads/financial_information/reports/2005/2005_annual_report.zip>, accessed 24 September 2008.

SIRAN (Social Investment Research Analyst Network) (2005), *A Call to Action: For Greater Corporate Transparency 10 years After the Glass Ceiling Commission Recommendations* (Washington DC: Social Investment Research Analyst Network). Available online at <http://www.siran.org/pdfs/calltoaction.pdf>.

Teather, D. (2006), 'Glass Ceiling Still Blocks Women from the Executive Floor,' *Guardian*, 2 October.

Tinker, T. and Neimark, M. (1987), 'The Role of Annual Reports in Gender and Class Contradictions at General Motors: 1917–1976', *Accounting, Organizations and Society*, 12: 71–88.

Tesco (2005), *Corporate Responsibility Review*, [online report], <http://www.tesco.com/csr/index.html>, accessed 10 October 2008.

Tonkin, D. J. and Skerrat, L. (eds) (1983), *Financial Reporting 1983–1984* (London: ICAEW).

Glass Ceiling Commission (1995). *A Solid Investment: Making Full Use of the Nation's Human Capital*, final report of the Commission (Washington DC: Government Printing Office). Available online at <http://digitalcommons.ilr.cornell.edu/key_workplace/120/>.

Vogel. D. (2005), *The Market for Virtue: the Potential and Limits of Corporate Social* Responsibility (Washington: Brookings Institution).

Wal-Mart (2005), *A Year of Accomplishments 2005: Office of Diversity* [online PDF report], <http://walmartwatch.com/img/documents/2005_DiversityReport.pdf>, accessed 23 September 2008.

Wal-Mart (2006), *Annual Report*, Notes to Consolidated Financial Statements: 42–4). <http://www.scribd.com/doc/287574/WalMart-2006-Annual-Report>, accessed 23 September 2008.

Westpac (2005), *2005 Concise Annual Report* [online PDF report], <http://www.westpac.com.au/manage/pdf.nsf/C0E1F921DB957819CA2570B40000830B/$File/WAR2005CONCISE.pdf?OpenElement>, accessed 23 September 2008.

Working Mother Media Inc (2008), *Working Mothers* [online magazine], <http://www.workingmother.com>, accessed 23 September 2008.